William Patton

Jesus of Nazareth

who was He? and what is He now?

William Patton

Jesus of Nazareth
who was He? and what is He now?

ISBN/EAN: 9783337255244

Printed in Europe, USA, Canada, Australia, Japan

Cover: Foto ©Lupo / pixelio.de

More available books at **www.hansebooks.com**

Hebrew Heroes.

JERUSALEM.

Frontispiece.

JESUS OF NAZARETH:

WHO WAS HE?

AND

WHAT IS HE NOW?

"THESE ARE WRITTEN, THAT YE MIGHT BELIEVE THAT JESUS IS THE CHRIST, THE SON OF GOD; AND THAT BELIEVING YE MIGHT HAVE LIFE THROUGH HIS NAME." — *John* xx. 31.

BY THE

REV. WILLIAM PATTON, D.D.

NEW YORK:
ROBERT CARTER AND BROTHERS,
530 BROADWAY.
1879.

CAMBRIDGE:
PRESSWORK BY JOHN WILSON & SON.

INTRODUCTION.

A CONCISE history of Jesus of Nazareth, embodying the prominent facts of His life, is needed for general circulation. To meet this necessity this volume has been prepared. The Lives of Christ written by eminent scholars are of great value. Their learning, their illustrations of scenes and places, as well as their discussions about the miracles and teachings of our Lord, commend them. Their size and cost, however, limit their circulation.

As this narrative necessarily introduces other personages, especially the witnesses of the resurrection, enough of their biography is given to make manifest their temperament and character, and thus to render their testimony the more impressive.

Who was Jesus of Nazareth? and what is He now? are questions vital to every human being. They deserve to be seriously pondered, and honestly and intelligently answered. It is not enough to say, He was the son of Mary; or the son of the Virgin Mary. It is not enough to say, He was conceived in the womb of the Virgin by the Holy Ghost, "the power of the Highest overshadowing," though this fact is unique and of unparalleled importance. Perfectly to answer these questions, a comprehensive view must be taken of His entire life, teachings, and works, as they are recorded upon the inspired page.

I have the fullest confidence in His diversified miracles as demonstrations of His Divine power and goodness. I regard His parables as unsurpassed in beauty, simplicity, and point, and His teachings as unmatched for elevation, dignity, and purity. His replies to the many entangling questions of His keen-witted enemies were terse, prompt, and exhaustive, with no mingling of human infirmity. All these concentrate their testimony, and tell us, in part, who and what Jesus of Nazareth was and is.

But these I leave in their massive and impressive grandeur. Their illustration would lead me into rich and instructive fields of thought, which would far transcend the limits I have fixed, and in some measure divert attention from the purpose I have in view. I therefore confine myself to some of the more salient facts of His human pilgrimage, as telling with unmistakable emphasis who Jesus of Nazareth was, and what He now is. I wish to consider, simply and devoutly, of the strange though bright incidents which cluster so richly around His annunciation and birth; His baptism, with the affirming voice from heaven; His temptation, unequalled in length and intensity, with its triumphant issues; His transfiguration, with its unearthly splendour and Divine testimonies; the supper, as the memorial monument of His dishonoured death; His agonies amid the deep shadows and enfolding darkness of the garden; His base betrayal and arrest; His trial, eminent for its mockery of justice; His crucifixion, so tragic and graphic; His burial, amid vigilant wrath and unconquerable love; His resurrection, the essential foundation-fact of the Christian religion; His ascension, when a cloud of brightness and glory received Him; His mediatorial kingdom, administered from His throne at the right hand of God; and, finally, the dispensation of His Spirit, His power among men, and the destined triumphs of His truth and love.

These and facts of kindred prominence discriminate Him from all other beings who have appeared upon the page of history. These render Him individual and unique. These place Him on the highest possible elevation, so that He stands out in lone but brilliant conspicuousness as the Son of God, the King of men.

It is not the dead, but the living Christ that is the true life of every Christian. "I am crucified with Christ: nevertheless I live; yet not I, but Christ liveth in me: and the life which I now live in the flesh I live by the faith of the Son of God, who loved me, and gave Himself for me."[1]

"We see Jesus, who was made a little lower than the angels for the suffering of death, crowned with glory and honour; that He by the grace of God should taste death for every man."[2]

My design in this volume is not so much apologetic as expository. I write not so much for sceptics as for sincere believers in the Christian religion and in the Bible as the inspired Word of God. My design is to fix the attention of my reader upon this series of incidents, all found in one short life; incidents such as never centred in

[1] Gal. ii. 20.   [2] Heb. ii. 9.

whole or in part in any other being; and thus to produce a firm conviction that Jesus of Nazareth, though born of the Virgin Mary, and therefore "the Son of man," but being conceived by the Holy Ghost, is "the Son of God," and that in this union of the human and the Divine natures in one person He is the atoning Saviour, the risen, and reigning Mediatorial King.

Praying for the blessing of God to accompany this volume, I commend it

"*To Zion's friends and mine.*"

W. P

THE HARMONY

OF THE EVANGELISTS

On the Topics of this Volume.

SUBJECT.	MATT.	MARK.	LUKE.	JOHN.
Annunciation to Mary—*Nazareth*	...	...	1: 26-38	...
Angel instructs Joseph—*Nazareth*	1: 18-25	...	...	...
Jesus born—*Bethlehem*	...	...	2: 1-7	...
Shepherds and Song of Angels—*Bethlehem*	...	...	2: 8-20	...
Circumcision of Jesus—*Bethlehem*	...	...	2: 21	...
Purification and testimony of Simeon and Anna — *Temple, Jerusalem*	...	...	2: 22-38	...
The Magi—*Jerusalem and Bethlehem*	2: 1-6 9-12	...	...	...
Holy Family's Flight to Egypt	2: 13-14	...	...	...
Herod's Cruelty	2: 15-18	...	...	...
Return of Jesus to Nazareth	2: 19-23	...	2: 39-40	...
In the Temple at Twelve Years old—*Jerusalem*	...	...	2: 41-52	...
The Genealogies	1: 1-17	...	3: 23-38	...
Baptism of Jesus—*Jordan*	3: 13-17	1: 9-11	3: 21-23	...
Testimony of John the Baptist—*Bethabara*	...	...	...	1: 19-34
The Temptation—*Desert of Judea*	4: 1-11	1: 12-13	4: 1-13	...
The Transfiguration—*Region of Cæsarea Philippi*	17: 1-13	9: 2-13	9: 28-36	...
The Lord's Memorial Supper—*Jerusalem*	26: 26-29	14: 22-25	22: 19-20	1 Cor. 11: 23-25
Agony in Gethsemane—*Mount of Olives*	26: 30, 36-46	14: 20, 32-42	22: 39-46	18: 1
Betrayed by Judas—*Gethsemane*	26: 47-56	14: 43-52	22: 47-53	18: 2-12
Jesus before Annas—*Jerusalem*	...	...	...	18: 13, 14 19-24
Jesus before Caiaphas and the Sanhedrim—*Jerusalem*	26: 57-58 69-75	14: 53-54 66: 72	22: 54-62	18: 13-18 25-27
Jesus before Pilate—*Jerusalem*	27: 1, 2, 11-14	15: 1-5	23: 1-5	18: 28-38
Jesus before Herod—*Jerusalem*	...	...	23: 6-12	...
Barabbas preferred—*Jerusalem*	27: 15-26	15: 6-15	23: 13-25	18: 39-46
Pilate scourges Jesus and delivers Him to the Jews—*Jerusalem*	27: 26-30	15: 15-19	...	19: 1-3

SUBJECT	MATT.	MARK.	LUKE.	JOHN.
Pilate seeks to release Jesus—*Jerusalem*	...	...	...	19: 4-16
Jesus led to Calvary—*Calvary*	27: 31-34	15: 20-23	23: 26-33	19: 16,17
Jesus crucified—*Calvary*	27: 35-38	15: 24-28	23: 33-38	19: 18-24
The Superscription—*Calvary*	27: 30	15: 26	23: 38	19: 19-21
Jesus mocked—*Calvary*	27: 39-42	15: 29-33	23: 35-37	...
The Penitent Thief—*Calvary.*	...	...	23: 39-43	...
Jesus commits His Mother to John—*Calvary*	...	...	...	19: 25-27
The Darkness, and Jesus dies—*Calvary*	27: 45-50	15: 33-37	23: 44-46	19: 28-30
Veil of Temple rent—*Temple*	27: 51	15: 38	23: 45	...
The Earthquake, and the Graves opened—*Jerusalem*	27: 51-53	...	...	...
Centurion's Testimony—*Calvary*	27: 54	15: 39	23: 47	...
The Women Witnesses—*Calvary*	27: 55-56	15: 40-41	...	...
Prophecy fulfilled—*Calvary*	...	...	...	19: 31-37
Pilate gives the Corpse to Joseph —*Calvary*	27: 57-58	15: 42-45	23: 50-52	19: 38
The Burial—*Calvary*	27: 59-60	15: 46	23: 53	19: 38-42
The Guarding the Sepulchre—*Calvary*	27: 62-66	...	...	...
The Women at the Funeral—*Calvary*	27: 61	15: 47	23: 55-56	
The Resurrection—*Calvary*	27: 2-4	...	...	...
The Women early at the Tomb—*Calvary*	28: 1	16: 2-4	24: 1-3	20: 1
What they saw and heard—*Calvary*	28: 5-7	16: 5-7	24: 4-8	20: 2
Return to the City—*Calvary*	28: 8-10	16: 8	24: 9-11	...
Peter and John run to the Tomb; John saw and believed—*Calvary*	...	...	24: 12	20: 3-10
Jesus seen by Mary Magdalene—*Calvary*	...	16: 9-11	...	20: 11-18
Report of Roman Guard—*Calvary*	28: 11-15	...	...	...
Jesus at Emmaus—*Emmaus*	...	16: 12-13	24: 13-35	...
Jesus appears to the Apostles, Thomas being absent—*Jerusalem*	...	16: 14-18	24: 36-49	20: 19-23
Jesus appears to the Apostles with Thomas—*Jerusalem*	...	...	...	20: 24-29
The Apostles see Jesus at the Sea of Tiberias—*Galilee*	28: 16	...	...	21: 1-24
Jesus meets Five Hundred—*Galilee*	28: 16-20	[1 Cor. 15: 6]	...	...
The Ascension	...	16: 19-20	24: 50-53	...
The Final Testimony	[Acts 9: 1-12]	...	...	20: 30-31

TABLE OF CONTENTS.

Chapter i.
BIRTH AND YOUTH OF JESUS.
Annunciation— Birth— Shepherds — Circumcision — Purification—Simeon — Anna—Magi — Flight to Egypt — Herod and the slaughter of innocents—Return to Nazareth—At twelve years old in the Temple—Beauty of person and Divine humanity... *p.* 1

Chapter ii.
THE SILENCE OF EIGHTEEN YEARS.
Filial obedience—Dignity of labour 39

Chapter iii.
THE BAPTISM AND PRIESTHOOD.
John the Baptist—John questioned by the priests and Levites—John's testimony at the Jordan—Baptized—Dove—Voice—Priesthood—Not Aaronic—Melchizedec 51

Chapter iv.
THE TEMPTATION.
Why led to be tempted—Prophecy—Nature of temptation or trial—Protracted temptation—Adam inexcusable—Jesus an example—Sympathising High Priest—Trials elevate—Christ's human nature tried—The wilderness—The fast—Sustained by miracle—Moses, Elijah—The Tempter a person—His agonies diverse ways—Through external organs—Mental laws—Association—Imagination—Curiosity — Cases — First parents—Job —

Jesus—First trial, hungered—Second trial, pinnacle of Temple—Third trial, all the kingdoms—Temptations through life—Warnings and hope—Armour—Truth, its power 71

Chapter v.
THE TRANSFIGURATION.

Mountains prominent in Scripture—Hermon—Peter, John, and James—Prayed, and countenance changed—Moses and Elias translated—Conversation—Sleep—Saw His glory—Cloud—Voice—Senseless as dead—Jesus touched them—Forbidden to tell of it till after the resurrection—Old and New Testament one 111

Chapter vi.
THE MEMORIAL SUPPER.

Monuments common—Of stone and metal to commemorate popular men and events, perishable—His a crucifixion as a malefactor—An ignominious death—Material bread and fruit of the vine 123

Chapter vii.
GETHSEMANE.

A garden—Disciples present—Christ alone—His prayer—The cup—What drops of blood—What He feared—Prayer answered—Heb. v. 7—Not die then and there—Angel strengthens ... 131

Chapter viii.
THE BETRAYAL.

Meets Judas—The soldiers fall to the ground—The kiss—Question—Jesus not deceived—Seized and bound—Peter and his sword—Miracle of healing—Carried away 149

Chapter ix.
THE TRIAL.

Before Annas, the former High Priest—Examined of His doctrine—Reply—Unlawfully smitten—Not reproved—Paul's case—Before Caiaphas—Pharisees take no part—False witnesses—Jesus holds His peace—Attempt to make Him convict Himself—Christ admits His Divinity—Clothes rent—Charged with blasphemy and guilty of death—Mocked—Spit upon—Blindfolded—Before Pilate—A Roman procurator—Not the most guilty—Calls for the accusation and dismisses the case—Return with accusation—Perverting nation, and refusing tribute—Examined—Christ's silence—Pilate further examines—What is truth?—No fault in Him—Sent to Herod—Fierce accusations by the priests—Questions—No proof—Silence of Christ—Set at naught and mocked—Sent back—Again before Pilate—Pronounced innocent—Proposed to chastise—Jesus or Barabbas—Christ rejected—Message from Pilate's wife—Barabbas chosen—Clamour for crucifixion—Pilate strives—Priests prevail—Washing his hands—Imprecation of Jews—Scourged—Soldiers cruelly treat, mock, and deride Him—Last attempt of Pilate—Blasphemy again charged—Christ's silence—Reply to Pilate—Political motives, and Pilate yields and gives the order—Led away—Bears His Cross—Daughters of Jerusalem—Calvary not a mountain—Place of execution—Two thieves—Crucifixion a Roman punishment—Stripped—Laid down on the cross—Prayer—Inscription—Jews dissatisfied—Cross raised up—Divide the clothes—Prophecy fulfilled—Bodily suffering—Reviled thieves—One prays—Christ promises—Mental sufferings—The darkness—Christianity born—Dies all alone, and with submission—Touching incident with His mother—Where He trusts His cause—The women—Veil rent—Scruples—Prophecy... 159

Chapter x.
THE BURIAL.

Actually dead—Evidence—Joseph of Arimathæa—Nicodemus—Roman guard—Loving women—Magdalene—Mary wife of Cleophas—Salome—Joanna 213

Chapter xi.
THE RESURRECTION.

Night—Earthquake—Angel—Guards—Time in the tomb—Women on the way—Mary Magdalene goes for Peter and John—Other women see the angel—See Jesus—His message—Tell Disciples—Peter and John come—John believed—Mary Magdalene does not recognise Christ—Afterwards she knows Him—Testimony of soldiers—Credibility of witnesses—Emmaus—Expounds Scriptures—Made known—With the Ten—Christ appears—Proofs—With the Ten and Thomas—Thomas's conduct—Convinced—Sea of Tiberias—Christ speaks to them—Talk with Peter—The five hundred—Other testimonies—Peter—Paul—What if no resurrection? 229

Chapter xii.
THE ASCENSION.

His teachings for forty days—Promise of the Spirit—Mount of Olives—Taken up—Cloud—His last act a benediction—Two men, and who were they—Prediction—Return to Jerusalem—Life of Jesus meets the prophecies... 285

Chapter xiii.
THE GIFT OF THE HOLY SPIRIT.

Apostles abide in Jerusalem praying—Holy Spirit given by Christ—The Spirit's power always present—A distinctive part of Christ's mission—Apostolic Preaching—Filled with faith and the Holy Ghost—Fundamentals—Jesus and the Resurrection—Pentecost—Other times... 295

Chapter xiv.
THE MEDIATORIAL KING.

Wherefore ascend?—Prophecy—History—To carry out all the purposes of the atonement—Every being interested—The heavenly principalities—Illustrates the nature of sin and rebel angels—Men under mercy—Government of God—Power of love—Consummation—Great majority saved—and Christ satisfied ... 309

I.

THE BIRTH AND YOUTH OF JESUS.

CHAPTER I.

THE BIRTH AND YOUTH OF JESUS.

THE ANNUNCIATION.

THE birth of Jesus Christ was attended by such peculiar circumstances, both private and public, as to give it very marked distinction. The more private circumstances were known in the immediate family and the wider circle of relatives. "The angel Gabriel was sent from God unto a city of Galilee, named Nazareth, to a virgin espoused to a man whose name was Joseph, of the house of David; and the virgin's name was Mary." "And the angel said unto her, Fear not, Mary: for thou hast found favour with God. And, behold, thou shalt conceive in thy womb, and bring forth a Son, and shalt call His name JESUS." "The

Holy Ghost shall come upon thee, and the power of the Highest shall overshadow thee: therefore also that holy thing which shall be born of thee shall be called the Son of God."[1] Here are facts to be clearly authenticated or denied. The name of the virgin and her residence are given, and the additional incident that she "was espoused to a man whose name was Joseph." Not any Joseph, but "Joseph of the house of David;" Joseph the lineal descendant from David the king; Joseph of the royal line. The appearance of the angel Gabriel and his wonderful announcement to the virgin doubtless were private, and known only to Mary and a few to whom she communicated the facts. They rest not alone on her veracity, but also on the corroborating circumstances of the birth of John the Baptist, whose mother Elisabeth, the wife of Zacharias, bore this son when she and her husband "were well stricken in years."[2]

THE BIRTH.

This did not take place at Nazareth, in Galilee, the residence of Joseph, but in

[1] Luke i. 26, 27, 30, 31, 35.   [2] Luke i. 18.

Bethlehem of Judea. This town was six miles south-west from Jerusalem and eighty miles from Nazareth. Though of great antiquity, it never was a place of political importance. It was, and is, illustrious chiefly as the birthplace of David and of Christ. In its neighbourhood stood the tomb of Rachel. In its fields Ruth gleaned. On its hills David watched his flocks. But that which gathers to it the interest of all the ages is the fact that Jesus was born there. " Now the birth of Jesus Christ was on this wise : "[1] "It came to pass in those days, that there went out a decree from Cæsar Augustus, that all the world should be taxed."[2] This enrolment was not carried out, in the usual Roman manner, in the cities where the people resided or in the district to whose jurisdiction the places of their abode belonged. But the emperor ordered them to appear according to families, it being usual to register the Jews in the town where the family originated. This concession to the Jews was made because of their intense sensitiveness as to any tax being levied upon them by a heathen power by which they had

---

[1] Matt. i. 18.   [2] Luke ii. 1.

been subjugated; as also because of the tenacity with which they held to their genealogies. Matthew thus sums up the genealogy by Joseph: "So all the generations from Abraham to David are fourteen generations; and from David until the carrying away into Babylon are fourteen generations; and from the carrying away into Babylon unto Christ are fourteen generations."[1] Luke (iii. 23-28) traces the genealogical line on the side of Mary. Thus both by Joseph and Mary Jesus was a lineal descendant of David. Dr. Edward Robinson, in his *Harmony*, says: "Matthew, as writing particularly for Jews, traces our Lord's descent only to David and to Abraham; but Luke, as writing for Gentiles, traces it rather to Adam. The two genealogies thus prove Jesus to be: 1. *The Son of David*, who should, according to promise, sit on the throne of Israel (Isa. ix. 6, 7; Luke i. 32; Acts ii. 30). 2. *The Seed of Abraham*, in whom all nations of the earth should be blessed, according to the covenant made with the father of the faithful (Gen. xxii. 18; Gal. iii. 14-16). 3. *The Son of Man*, or, 'the seed of the

[1] Matt. i. 17.

woman,' who should bruise the serpent's head (Gen. iii. 15; Heb. ii. 14)." The enrolment being made in Bethlehem, in accordance with Jewish usage, would be an authoritative recognition of the royal descent of Jesus both by Joseph and by Mary.

"All went to be taxed, every one into his own city. And Joseph also went up from Galilee, out of the city of Nazareth, into Judea, unto the city of David, which is called Bethlehem; (because he was of the house and lineage of David:) to be taxed with Mary his espoused wife, being great with child."[1] It was the Roman custom to number the women and children as well as the men, and therefore Mary, notwithstanding her then condition, accompanied Joseph. But from the genealogy as given by Luke there is ground for the belief that Mary went to be enrolled as the heiress of another branch of David's family. In obedience to this decree of the Roman emperor the prophecy of Micah v. 2 was fulfilled: "But thou, Bethlehem Ephratah, though thou be little among the thousands of Judah, yet out of thee shall

[1] Luke ii. 3–5.

He come forth unto Me that is to be ruler in Israel." This prediction was understood as referring to the Messiah. Those who rejected Him because of His residence in Galilee said, "Shall Christ come out of Galilee? Hath not the Scripture said, That Christ cometh of the seed of David, and out of the town of Bethlehem, where David was?"[1] Thus does Providence always answer truly to prophecy.

The enrolment drew many strangers to this little town, in which there was but one khan, or inn. So that when Joseph and Mary arrived " there was no room for them in the inn." Necessity compelled them to seek the next best shelter. There " was attached to this inn a stable or court for cattle, having a partial shelter and a bench, or perhaps a trough, for provender, here called a manger."

Tradition, on the authority of some of the fathers, says that it was a cave. Caves, we know, were often used as stables. But as the inspired record is silent on this point, we prefer to adhere to the simple statement that the infant Saviour was laid in a manger to which the cattle resorted for their food.

[1] John vii. 41, 42.

"Among the hay and straw spread for the food and rest of the cattle, weary with their day's journey, far from home, in the midst of strangers, in the chilly winter night — in circumstances so devoid of all earthly comfort or splendour that it is impossible to imagine a humbler nativity — Christ was born."[1] "And so it was, that, while they were there, the days were accomplished that she should be delivered. And she brought forth her first-born Son, and wrapped Him in swaddling clothes, and laid Him in a manger; because there was no room for them in the inn."[2] How long the mother, with the Holy Child, remained in this cattle enclosure is not intimated. Probably it was not long, as the many strangers, having accomplished their enrolment, would depart, leaving better accommodation for the Holy Family; as by the Jewish law the mother could not leave the house for forty days.

THE SHEPHERDS.

The next incident connected with the birth of the Saviour is the announcement made by

---

[1] Farrar's *Life of Christ*.   [2] Luke ii. 6, 7.

an angel to the shepherds, who, in the district of Bethlehem, were keeping the watches of the night over their flock: "Lo, the angel of the Lord came upon them, and the glory of the Lord shone round about them." This unexpected and overpowering splendour not only surprised but alarmed them: "they were sore afraid." Allaying their fears, "the angel said unto them, I bring you good tidings of great joy, which shall be to all people. For unto you is born this day in the city of David a Saviour, which is Christ the Lord."[1] These three appellations — Saviour, Christ, Lord — point to His saving work, His Divine appointment as the Anointed One, and His supreme dignity as Mediatorial King. The sign or evidence which was to confirm their faith in this announcement was the fact, "Ye shall find the babe wrapped in swaddling clothes, lying in a manger." Immediately, yea, "suddenly there was with the angel a multitude of the heavenly host praising God, and saying, Glory to God in the highest, and on earth peace, good will toward men."[2] Such was the historic song of the

[1] Luke ii. 9-11 [2] Luke ii. 13, 14.

angels celebrating the incarnation of Messiah, when "the Word was made flesh, and dwelt among us."[1]

When the angels had departed and the last echo of their song had died away, the shepherds went in haste to Bethlehem, where they "found Mary, and Joseph, and the babe lying in a manger." They saw the appointed sign, and believed. Then "they made known abroad the saying which was told them concerning this child." Those who heard wondered, but "Mary kept [in memory] all these things, and pondered in her heart." Having performed their mission to the city of David, the shepherds returned to their vigils over their flocks, but with hearts full, for they praised and glorified God "for all the things that they had heard and seen, as it was told unto them." All these strange but significant facts cluster like stars of light around the birth of Christ.

THE CIRCUMCISION.

In obedience to the command, " Every man child among you shall be circumcised," " He that is eight days old shall be circumcised,"[2]

---

[1] John i. 14.   [2] Gen. xvii. 10, 12.

the infant Saviour was circumcised, and "His name was called JESUS."[1] The conferring of this name was neither accidental nor in the ordinary course of things. So far as the two genealogies are given, there is no evidence that any of His kindred bore that name. It was given Him by Divine appointment. "Which was so named of the angel before He was conceived in the womb." So also an angel told Joseph, "Thou shalt call His name JESUS: for He shall save His people from their sins." Jesus was the proper name of our Lord, and to distinguish Him from others He is also called "Jesus of Nazareth" and "Jesus the Son of Joseph." Jesus is the English modification of the Greek form of the name. Its import is indicated by the reason assigned by the angel to Joseph, "because *He shall save* His people from their sins." Christ is not a proper name, but a designation of office, "the anointed." Instead of saying *Jesus Christ*, it is more accurate to say *Jesus the Christ*. "The Messiah" and "the Christ" (words of the same meaning in two different languages) designate

[1] Luke ii. 21.

His office as the Anointed Prophet, Priest, and King.

As the mother, according to the Jewish law, could not leave the house for forty days, the circumcision was doubtless performed by Joseph at Bethlehem. The narrative gives no further prominence to this event than the simple record of the fact that, in strict accordance with the legal requirement, He was circumcised on the eighth day.

THE PURIFICATION.

By the law, from the time of the birth of a male child, the mother was held to be unclean for forty days; during which time she was not allowed to leave the house. Accordingly, on the fortieth day the virgin mother, with her babe, presented herself at the Temple for purification.

The prescribed offering was "a lamb of the first year for a burnt offering, and a young pigeon, or a turtle dove, for a sin offering," which the priest shall offer "before the Lord, and make an atonement for her; and she shall be cleansed." But if the parent, through poverty, was unable to present the lamb, "then she shall bring two turtles, or two young pigeons; the one for the burnt offering, and the other for a sin offering, and the priest shall make an atonement for her, and she shall be clean."[1] It was with this offering, clearly denoting the humble pecuniary condition of Joseph, that Mary presented herself for purification.

Under the law God claimed the first-born as peculiarly His, to be devoted to the Temple service. As all such would not be required, a provision for redemption was instituted: "Nevertheless the first-born of man shalt thou surely redeem" "for the money of five shekels, after the shekel of the sanctuary."[2] The amount of the redemption in English coin would be about sixteen shillings.

By His circumcision the Lord was formally "placed under the law," and subjected to all its demands. So teaches the apostle: "But when the fulness of the time was come, God sent forth His Son, made of a woman, made under the law, to redeem them that were under the law, that we might receive the adoption of sons."[3]

[1] Lev. xii. 6–3. [2] Num. xviii. 15, 16. [3] Gal. iv. 4, 5.

This presentation of the babe at the Temple was deepened in significance by the recognition of this infant as the promised Messiah—the Saviour—by Simeon, "a just and devout man, waiting for the consolation of Israel;" and by Anna, a prophetess, who "served God with fastings and prayers." The Holy Ghost was upon Simeon, "and it was revealed unto him by the Holy Ghost, that he should not see death, before he had seen the Lord's Christ;" "the Lord's Anointed One." Under the influence and guidance of the Spirit, he came into the Temple—he took the babe "up in his arms, and blessed God, and said, Lord, now lettest Thou Thy servant depart in peace, according to Thy word: for mine eyes have seen Thy salvation, which Thou hast prepared before the face of all people; a light to lighten the Gentiles, and the glory of Thy people Israel."[1] These wonderful utterances, forecasting the future greatness and blessedness of this child, deeply amazed Joseph and the mother: they "marvelled at those things which were spoken of Him." Simeon then "blessed them." To

[1] Luke ii. 25-32.

Mary he said, "This child is set for the fall and rising again of many in Israel; and for a sign which shall be spoken against." It is not a life of peace and triumph and glory which is before Him, but of opposition and strife, of suffering and sorrow, of betrayal and death. "Yea, a sword shall pierce through thy own soul also;" fulfilled most solemnly when, with tearless anguish, she saw Him nailed to the cross.

Anna the prophetess,[1] a widow aged about eighty-four years, who "departed not from the Temple, but served God... night and day," "coming in at that instant gave thanks likewise unto the Lord, and spake of Him to all them that looked for redemption in Jerusalem." Perverted as were the ideas of the Sanhedrim, who looked for a temporal conquering prince in the promised Messiah, and general as were the corruptions of the times, still there was a remnant of the truly pious in the Holy City who searched and understood the Scriptures, and who encouraged each other whilst looking for the promised One.

[1] Luke ii. 36.

The attestation of Simeon is corroborative of the fact that the Jews, as instructed by the prophets, were at that time expecting the appearance of the Messiah. It is more than this. The facts, that "it was revealed unto him by the Holy Ghost, that he should not see death, before he had seen the Lord's Christ," that he came by the Spirit into the Temple, and that he immediately recognised the babe as the promised Saviour, carry the Divine attestation that this Jesus is the Son of God, the Divine Redeemer, the "Lamb of God which taketh away the sin of the world."

THE MAGI.

Incidents of intense interest crowd forward to add their testimony. We have heard from the devout in Israel that the Messiah had come, "a light to lighten the Gentiles;" and now a deputation of wise men from the Gentile world of the East come to pay their homage.

These wise men, in their own country, supposed to be Chaldæa, were called Magi. They were men of distinction, as the leaders in religion and learned in astronomy and astrology. At this time, throughout the East, there was a prevailing, and in some parts an intense, conviction that a powerful king would arise in Judea, who would obtain dominion over the whole world. The way in which this expectation originated and spread may be accounted for with a measurable degree of certainty. Suetonius says: "An old and firm opinion had prevailed over all the East that it was written in the Book of the Fates that some one coming out of Judea at that time should obtain the empire of the world." Among the Jews this looking for a conqueror to deliver their nation and to have supreme authority, took its rise from the prophecies concerning the Messiah contained in their sacred books. Josephus intimates that among the Arabians, who descended from Ishmael, it was derived from the promise made to Abraham. Of this promise they preserved a traditional knowledge. Balaam, the Arabian, when importuned by Balak to curse Israel, said, " There shall come a Star out of Jacob, and a Sceptre shall rise out of Israel, and shall smite the corners of Moab, and destroy all the children of Sheth." "Out of Jacob shall come He that shall have dominion." The Septuagint version is: "A man shall come forth of his [Jacob's] seed, and shall rule many nations, and his kingdom shall be exalted above Gog [the name of the kings of the Scythian nations], and it shall be increased." The Jews, who in their several captivities were dispersed through the East, spread the knowledge of their prophecies of the Messiah, and thus begat that expectation which was so universal as to attract the notice of Tacitus, the Roman historian. Zoroaster, the reformer of discipline and worship in Persia, is maintained by many to have been a disciple of the prophet Daniel, whose predictions concerning the Messiah were most definite as to the time of His appearing. Thus was accomplished the prophecy in Haggai (ii. 7), "I will shake all nations, and the Desire of all nations shall come: and I will fill this house with glory, saith the Lord of Hosts."

The Magi noticed a new star, or luminous appearance, in the heavens, which, according to the then received doctrine, they recognised as the symbol of a new kingly power. What this star was cannot now be determined, but the design of its appearance is made manifest. Perceiving that it moved not as other stars did, but appeared to advance in a westerly course, they followed as it led the way, and, with its light upon their path, arrived at Jerusalem. Naturally and with propriety they presented themselves to Herod, then the king under the Roman empire, with the inquiry, "Where is He that is born King of the Jews?" To give point and force to this question they state, "For we have seen His star in the east, and are come to worship Him." This question and these testimonies troubled Herod, "and all Jerusalem with him." Herod being an Idumæan, a foreigner and a usurper, had good cause to fear one who by birth was King of the Jews. All Jerusalem reasonably dreaded fresh conflicts and wars, which would certainly lead to new and perhaps more aggravated cruelties on the part of Herod. The king, concealing his apprehensions, treated the Magi with respect, and having heard their request, he "gathered all the chief priests and scribes of the people together," and "demanded of them where

Christ should be born."[1] The highest intelligence, learning, and authority were thus convened; and the scribes, from a careful examination of their sacred books, replied, "In Bethlehem of Judea." The apprehension and trouble of Herod were not allayed, but intensified, by this answer. It woke up new determinations, as the place of the nativity was in his own dominions and near at hand. "Herod, when he had privily called the wise men, inquired of them diligently what time the star appeared." Knowing this, he could form a probable estimate of the time when this King of the Jews was born. He then sent the Magi to Bethlehem, with the injunction, "Go and search diligently for the young child; and when ye have found Him, bring me word again, that I may come and worship Him also." The charge to "search diligently" arose from the belief that the parents of the Messiah would conceal Him until He should grow to manhood. If he had formed the purpose of killing this child, he covered it up with the proffered desire to worship Him; another illustration of the truth that there are more hypocrites out of the Church than there are in it.

[1] Matt. ii. 4.

When the Magi had received the instructions of Herod, "they departed; and, lo, the star, which they saw in the east, went before them, till it came and stood over where the young Child was." Thus guided, "they rejoiced with exceeding great joy. And when they were come into the house, they saw the young Child with Mary His mother, and fell down, and worshipped Him." The phrase "fell down" indicates that, according to the custom of Eastern people, they did not simply kneel, but prostrated themselves on the ground, and in this humble attitude did homage to the Child, thus acknowledging Him as King and offering allegiance to Him. As Eastern people never come into the presence of their prince without an offering, which generally consists of the choicest productions of their country, so the Magi "opened their treasures," and "presented unto Him gifts; gold, and frankincense, and myrrh." This was the highest tribute they could pay. Notwithstanding the humble condition in which they found Him, they manifested a reverence which we do not read they had paid to Herod, who dwelt in his magnificent palace.

The visit of these "wise men from the east," so singularly led to Bethlehem by the guiding star, was not one of mere ceremony, but designed of God to make clear to all the generations of men what were the expectations then entertained among the Gentiles, and to confirm the prophecies which had raised such a general hope—"the Desire of all nations." Their coming brought out under positive authority the decision of the Sanhedrim, embracing the most learned of the Jewish teachers of the law then living, that Bethlehem was to be the place of their Messiah's nativity. The return of these "wise men" to their own country would carry tidings of the Messiah, which would prepare the way for the reception of the Gospel when it should be carried thither by the apostles of the Lord. Nor can we overlook the beneficent care of Providence in the gifts of these "wise men," thus placing Joseph in a condition to support his family in Egypt, whither he was to flee to preserve the life of the Child.

Though Herod succeeded in covering up his designs respecting the babe "born King of the Jews" from the knowledge of men, he could not deceive God. Knowing perfectly his cruel purpose, He warned the wise men not to return to Jerusalem and give information to Herod, but to depart to their country by another route. This they obeyed. As all God's plans are harmonious, and work together as parts of a whole, He sent an angel who appeared to Joseph in a dream or vision, saying, "Arise, and take the young Child and His mother, and flee into Egypt, and be thou there until I bring thee word: for Herod will seek the young Child to destroy Him." Thus warned, and stimulated by the reason assigned, Joseph immediately complied. "When he arose, he took the young Child and His mother by night, and departed into Egypt." Both Egypt and Syria were beyond the dominion of Herod. Egypt was nearer to Bethlehem than was Syria. Herod had less of influence in Egypt than in Syria. In Egypt, and particularly at Alexandria, there were many Jews, by whom Joseph and his family would be welcomed, and with whom they could reside in safety. But in whatever place they abode, it was the place of refuge which God had provided for them. How long they lived in Egypt is not stated. The limitation was until the death of Herod.

Having waited in vain for the return of the wise men, and having failed in obtaining definite information of the time of the birth and the place of residence of the Child "born King of the Jews," Herod "was exceeding wroth," and now determined to secure his object by a wide slaughter. He "sent forth, and slew all the [male] children that were in Bethlehem, and in all the coasts thereof, from two years old and under, according to the time which he had diligently inquired of the wise men." He had ascertained from the Magi when they first saw the star, and how long they had been on their journey, and thus concluded that from two years and under would certainly include this particular child. "All the coasts thereof" were brought under this curse, lest the child might not be in Bethlehem, but be secreted in the neighbourhood. These instructions to his agents show how intensely determined he was to destroy the Child "born King of the Jews." That this massacre of the innocents was accomplished is a fact well authenticated. The evangelist chronicles the event as the fulfilment of a prediction: "Then was fulfilled that which was spoken by Jeremy the prophet, saying, In Rama was there a voice heard, lamentation, and weeping, and great mourning, Rachel weeping for her children, and would not be comforted, because they are not."[1] How many children were thus slaughtered cannot now be determined; only a probable estimate can be made. Bethlehem, it is known, was not a large place, and consequently the number of children under two years could not be numerous, probably not more than twenty-five or thirty. This act of cruelty, dictated by political motives, was in perfect keeping with the character of the man who murdered his wife, his brother, his three sons, and who ordered a general massacre for the day of his funeral, so that his body might be buried, not amidst rejoicings, but amidst the tears and lamentations of the people for their own dead.

Soon after this terrible and vengeful act

[1] Matt. ii. 17, 18.

of cruelty Herod died. Then an angel of the Lord appeared "in a dream [or vision] to Joseph in Egypt, saying, Arise, and take the young Child and His mother, and go into the land of Israel: for they are dead which sought the young Child's life." Joseph "took the young Child and His mother, and came into the land of Israel," intending, most probably, to return to Bethlehem, that he might there suitably educate this son, so singularly pointed out as the promised Messiah. " But when he heard," on his reaching the southern part of Judea, " that Archelaus did reign in Judea in the room of his father Herod, he was afraid to go thither," and " turned aside into the parts of Galilee." This part of Palestine was under the dominion of Herod Antipas, who, though own brother to Archelaus, was a man of milder temperament. Here Joseph thought that, in the obscurity of his humble occupation, and in a village distant from Jerusalem, this son would be more safe from the atrocities of wicked, ambitious men. "And he came and dwelt in a city called Nazareth," a small town in Lower Galilee, about eighty miles from Jerusalem and six miles north-west of Mount Tabor, and midway between the river Jordan and the Mediterranean Sea. The evangelist Luke thus closes this part of the life of our Lord: "And when they had performed all things according to the law of the Lord, they returned into Galilee, to their own city Nazareth. And the child grew, and waxed strong in spirit, filled with wisdom: and the grace of God was upon Him."[1] The statement that "He increased in wisdom and stature" can only apply to His human nature, which was complete and distinct from the Divine. This, and only this, was capable of growth in wisdom, and could be dependent upon Divine influences.

The union of Divinity with humanity in the person of Jesus Christ no man can explain, and no man can comprehend. How the finite and the infinite, the human and the Divine, were so united in Christ as to form one complex person, the Scriptures do not explain. They simply reveal and state the fact as a matter of faith, without any attempt to solve the mystery of the incarnation. That such an union of the human

[1] Luke ii. 39, 40.

and Divine in one Person existed we must believe, because it rests on evidence clear and abundant, and which cannot be set aside. The fact may be and is clear, whilst the method of the union is incomprehensible to our present limited faculties ; not more inexplicable, however, than the union of the soul, a spiritual existence, with the fleshly human body. By what subtle arrangement the soul indwells and gives life and power to the body, no investigation of men has ever detected. The fact is palpable, but the explanation lies beyond our reach. So the union of the human and the Divine in Christ, forming one Person, is a fact.

AT TWELVE YEARS OF AGE.

The law required the presence of all males thrice a year in the Holy City, to celebrate the appointed festivals. When Jesus was twelve years old the parents took Him with them to Jerusalem. Among the Jews, when a boy, entered his thirteenth year he was called a " son of the law," and was initiated into its observances. At this visit an incident occurred which is the more remarkable as it is the only piece of intelligence recorded in that period of Christ's life which extended from the presentation in the Temple to His baptism, covering a period of about thirty years. "And when they had fulfilled the days, as they returned, the child Jesus tarried behind in Jerusalem; and Joseph and His mother knew not of it." When the Passover ended, a great number of strangers, forming themselves into companies for companionship and security, would leave the city for their respective homes. The parents, supposing that Jesus was somewhere in the company, felt no apprehension. But when, at the close of the first day's journey, they "sought Him among their kinsfolk and acquaintance," and "found Him not," they were filled with anxiety, and immediately, though the day was deepening into night, "they turned back again to Jerusalem, seeking Him." Maternal love made Mary intrepid. She pressed on through the dark and lonely way with eager search. On the third day, to their great joy, "they found Him in the Temple, sitting in the midst of the doctors, both hearing them, and asking them questions."[1] The

---

[1] Luke ii. 46.

fact that He was found in the Temple—found where the learned doctors of the law gave their interpretations, may not be regarded as strange for an intelligent youth of inquiring mind. But that a person so young should understandingly enter into the discussions of these learned men, and evince such depth of thought, was a matter of marvel. "All that heard Him were astonished at His understanding and answers." So also were the parents amazed. It is, however, prominent on the face of the narrative, that Jesus was there to inquire and learn. There was in His manner neither forwardness nor arrogance, which would have been rebuked by the teachers of the law. But the utmost freedom of inquiry and discussion was encouraged by the learned. The mother, with something of reproach, said, " Son, why hast Thou thus dealt with us? behold, Thy father and I have sought Thee sorrowing." His answer is memorable for its simplicity and earnestness. These are the first recorded words of the Lord Jesus: " How is it that ye sought Me? wist ye not that I must be about My Father's business?" This reply indicates great maturity of mind, thirst for knowledge, a love of truth, and faith in the being, presence, and favour of God. More than this, it reveals the consciousness of His Divine nature and mission. It is in perfect keeping with what He said at the well of Samaria, "My meat is to do the will of Him that sent Me, and to finish His work."[1] There is perhaps an implied surprise that, after the annunciation made by Gabriel to Mary, the strange manifestations at the birth, the attestations of Simeon and Anna at the purification, and the homage of the wise men from the East, Joseph and Mary should still be in doubt about His Divine nature and mission. But they did not comprehend the past. "And they understood not the saying which He spake unto them." "His mother kept all these sayings in her heart." Though she could not then understand the full meaning of these things, she did not reject or disbelieve them; she thought upon them, and waited for their development. Though conscious of His Divine parentage as "the Son of God," yet, in dutiful obedience, "He went down with them, and came to

[1] John iv. 34.

Nazareth, and was subject unto them." This cheerful and prompt subjection showed itself in obedience to parental authority and in working at the trade of Joseph. We read that those who in Nazareth rejected Him said, " Is not this the carpenter, the son of Mary?"[1]

The desire to know the early history of Jesus is quite natural. But an almost impenetrable screen is thrown over it. So far as the incidents of His life bear upon the great work for which He became incarnate, they are clearly stated. The only recorded particulars prior to His entrance upon His public ministry are,—the annunciation and the circumstances of His birth, His circumcision and presentation in the Temple, with the facts that at the age of twelve He distinguished Himself among the learned doctors by a wisdom and penetration far in advance of His years, and that He thus early understood the Divine purpose of His mission on earth. The narrative contains nothing for the gratification of curiosity; it furnishes no details of life, no incidents of adventure; it tells only that

[1] Mark vi. 3.

"He increased in wisdom and stature, and in favour with God and man." These statements refer to His human nature. His wisdom and stature are both especially mentioned, as if His bodily no less than His mental development was remarkable. Is it, then, a stretch of imagination to say that, whilst He remained with His mother in Nazareth, the comeliness of His person, the sweetness of His disposition, and the vigour of His faculties, contributed to win the admiration and affection of all who were acquainted with Him? "Thou art fairer than the children of men: grace is poured into Thy lips: therefore God hath blessed Thee for ever."[1] In His human person He made manifest the excellency and glory of a being made in the image of God and sinless. But when that same glorious One "bore our griefs and carried our sorrows,"—"was wounded for our transgressions and bruised for our iniquities"—"when His soul was made an offering for sin,"—no wonder that "His visage was so marred more than any man, and His form more than the sons of men!"

[1] Psa. xlv. 2.

In His youth and manhood were seen, undoubtedly, the personal beauty and grandeur of a sinless human being; while in the marred visage, so that there was "no comeliness" and "no beauty," were beheld the withering power of sin upon the body, even of a sinless person, when that person stood in the sinner's place, and " the iniquity of us all" was "laid upon Him." "Thou art not yet fifty years old,"[1] said the Jews on one occasion. The words read like a conjecture as to what was about His age. *Not fifty!* No, He was little more than *thirty* yet; but it was as though the overshadowing sorrow which He had come to endure had already enstamped upon His very form the characters of on-coming age. And so it is expressly said by the evangelist, that even while He went about doing good, the words of the prophet were receiving fulfilment: "Himself took our infirmities, and bare our sicknesses."[2]

The only additional fact of which we catch a glimpse is that Jesus had not the advantages of what was then accounted a superior edu-

[1] John viii. 57.   [2] Matt. viii. 17.

cation from the tuition of some distinguished teacher. Had His parents returned from Egypt to Bethlehem, He would most probably have been placed by them under the tuition of some illustrious Rabbi. But the careful providence of God, for wise reasons, directed matters otherwise. It was no part of the Divine plan that Jesus should owe anything to the teachings of the learned among the Jews. Carried in His infancy to Nazareth, He abode there, and was reared to manhood with only those intellectual advantages which that place afforded. Still, His mental powers were wonderfully developed. By His intimate acquaintance with the Sacred Scriptures and comprehensive understanding of Divine truth, He amazed the people who heard His teaching. When He taught in the synagogue at Nazareth, the people "were astonished, and said, Whence hath this man this wisdom? Is not this the carpenter's son? Is not His mother called Mary?" When He taught in the Temple, "the Jews marvelled, saying, How knoweth this man letters, having never learned?"[1]

[1] Matt. xiii. 54, 55; John vii. 15.

II.

THE SILENCE OF EIGHTEEN YEARS.

CHAPTER II.

THE SILENCE OF EIGHTEEN YEARS.

FROM the transaction in the Temple, for full eighteen years, there is an unbroken silence. For this silence through the greater part of His youth and manhood no reason is recorded. This has sometimes perplexed devout Christians. They cannot understand why so large a portion of His life on earth should be wrapped in such perfect seclusion. It is in vain to allow the imagination to play around this subject, and to suppose reasons, of the probability, much less the certainty, of which we can have no assurance. The only available light thrown upon these eighteen years is gathered from the incidental hints which crop out in the narrative of the evangelists, and, perhaps, from the fact that Christ had come as the true High Priest, taken in connexion with the requirements of the law concerning priesthood. True, He was not according to "the order of Aaron," nor "the law of a carnal commandment;" and yet it is interesting to trace any parallels between His priestly office and that which of old had been ordained by God. Now no priest could enter upon his office until he had reached his thirtieth year. "From thirty years old and upward until fifty years old shalt thou number them."[1] In like manner our Lord refrained from entering upon His public ministry until He was thirty years old, remaining in Nazareth, "subject to His parents."

The Scriptures make no secret of the humble social position of Jesus. Joseph, the husband of Mary, was a working carpenter. He dwelt in the little village of Nazareth, so inconsiderable, at least—if of no worse reputation—as to be held in contempt, not only in Jerusalem, but also in the towns of Galilee. When Philip said unto Nathanael, "We have found Him, of

[1] Num. iv. 23.

whom Moses in the law, and the prophets, did write, Jesus of Nazareth, the son of Joseph," in amazement Nathanael immediately exclaimed, "Can any good thing come out of Nazareth?" This was the place which lent its despised name to the scornful title written upon His cross, "Jesus of Nazareth, the King of the Jews." This was the home of our Lord for all but about three years of His life.

The humiliations and the burdens of poverty which Christ endured give to honest poverty a singular sacredness and dignity. The fact incidentally appears, that the larger portion of the life of Jesus was spent in humble manual labour. "Is not this the carpenter, the son of Mary?" Thus by His own example He proclaimed, with an emphasis which none other possibly could, the dignity of honest labour. Nay, more, with this He shows that honest hand-labour dignifies all those who are faithful in the station in which Providence places them. The fact that Jesus of Nazareth was a working carpenter till He was thirty years of age significantly rebukes all those who look down with scorn and contempt upon the labouring man who honestly earns his bread, and thus supports his family. This Jesus, the working carpenter, "thought it not robbery to be equal with God, took upon Him the form of a servant, humbled Himself, and became obedient unto death, even the death of the cross," that He might save even those who despise labour and the labourer. "For ye know the grace of our Lord Jesus Christ, that, though He was rich, yet for your sakes He became poor, that ye through His poverty might be rich."

> "Thirty years, unknown, I trod
> Galilee's sequestered sod;
> But My life was known to God.
>
> Daily work at Joseph's call,
> Daily life, with duties small,—
> Yet I was the Lord of all."

The phrase "subject to them" is a clear indication that Jesus submitted Himself to the control of His parents, not only in the days of His helpless infancy, but through all His boyhood and early manhood, up to the day when He entered upon the special work for which He became incarnate. By His prompt and cheerful obedience He would not only promote their temporal comfort, but secure their daily happiness. We have here a beautiful example of filial obedience, and the most impressive enforcement of this sacred duty. "Honour thy father and thy mother;" "Ye shall fear every man his mother, and his father;" "Honour thy father and thy mother, as the Lord thy God hath commanded thee."[1] Disobedience to parents is a sin which ensures the Divine wrath. "Cursed be he that setteth light by his father or his mother."[2] As the family is the foundation of all well-ordered civil society, and as obedience is the essential element of all peaceful government, the inspired apostle has made filial obedience a universal duty: "Children, obey your parents in the Lord: for this is right. Honour thy father and mother; which is the first commandment with promise; that it may be well with thee." "Children, obey your parents in all things: for this is well pleasing unto the Lord."[3] In this respect also we have the example of Jesus, enforced by another

---

[1] Exod. xx. 12; Lev. xix. 3; Deut. v. 16.
[2] Deut. xxvii. 16.
[3] Ephes. vi. 1, 2; Col. iii. 20.

apostle as the great rule of life: "Leaving us an example, that ye should follow His steps."[1]

The Scriptures favour us with another instructive glimpse by which we learn more of the conduct of our Lord during those years over which the veil is so closely drawn. Immediately after His temptation "Jesus returned in the power of the Spirit into Galilee." "And He came to Nazareth, where He had been brought up: and, as His custom was, He went into the synagogue on the sabbath day, and stood up for to read."[2]

Mark the words,—"As His custom was." This incidental phrase carries our thoughts back into the years over which the veil is spread. During these years He was faithful in His attendance upon the public worship of God. His youth and early manhood were exemplary. As often as the Sabbath returned, and the doors of the synagogue were opened, Jesus was found in His place there.

When advanced to maturity, according to the custom of the day, He would in His turn

[1] 1 Pet. ii. 21.   [2] Luke iv. 14, 16.

"stand up for to read," and take part in the public service. On this particular occasion there was delivered to Him the book of the prophet Esaias, and when He had opened the book He found the place where it is written, "The Spirit of the Lord is upon Me."[1] "And He began to say unto them, This day is this scripture fulfilled in your ears."[2]

He who said unto John the Baptist, "It becometh us to fulfil all righteousness," was doubtless faultless, both in form and spirit, in His careful obedience to all the requirements of the law. The command was peremptory: "Three times in the year all thy males shall appear before the Lord God."[3] "Three times in a year shall all thy males appear before the Lord thy God in the place which He shall choose; in the feast of unleavened bread, and in the feast of weeks, and in the feast of tabernacles."[4] To rebuke the fear that, the land being thus left defenceless, their enemies would seek upon these occasions to despoil them, the Divine promise was given:

[1] Isa. lxi. 1–3.   [2] Luke iv. 21.
[3] Exod. xxiii. 17.   [4] Deut. xvi. 16.

"Neither shall any man desire thy land, when thou shalt go up to appear before the Lord thy God thrice in the year."[1] The people's confidence was fortified by the assurance that there was no danger of loss whilst cheerfully obeying the command to worship God. We can scarcely doubt that Jesus was obedient, and that He, unostentatiously, regularly appeared among the multitude with the appointed sacrificial offerings. A specific ordinance says, "They shall not appear before the Lord empty."[2] "And none shall appear before Me empty."[3] The requirement was, "An half shekel shall be the offering of the Lord. The rich shall not give more, and the poor shall not give less."[4] This tribute was the ransom of the soul. The amount raised was for the service of the Tabernacle.[5] It was a memorial to make atonement. Thus benevolence and worship were united. In this our Lord failed not. The apostle Paul shows that in Christianity also, the union of benevolence and worship is obligatory. "Upon the first day of the week let every one of you

---

[1] Exod. xxxiv. 24. [2] Deut. xvi. 16. [3] Exod. xxiii. 15.
[4] Exod. xxx. 13, 15. [5] Exod. xxx. 16.

lay by him in store, as God hath prospered him, that there be no gatherings when I come." [1]

The eighteen silent years, then, are not barren of instructiveness. They teach us, as nothing else can, the dignity of manual labour, the beauty and value of filial obedience, and the importance of regular attendance upon public worship, with readiness to bear our part in its maintenance by our contributions and personal service. To our Lord, in His human nature, these were years of discipline, obedience, and patient waiting.

The first recorded public utterance of our Lord, when entering upon the veiled eighteen years, had been, " Wist ye not that I must be about My Father's business?" [2] When He next appears, His language is, " It becometh us to fulfil all righteousness." After He had entered upon His public ministry, He said, " I have a baptism to be baptized with." It was the baptism of blood. "And how am I straitened (pained) till it be accomplished!" [3] On the mountain, when transfigured, when "the fashion of His countenance

---

[1] 1 Cor. xvi. 2. [2] Luke ii. 49. [3] Luke xii. 50.

was altered," "when Moses and Elias appeared in glory" and talked with Him, the absorbing topic of their discourse was "His decease, which He should accomplish at Jerusalem."[1] Knowing that He came on earth to die upon the cross, "when the time was come that He should be received up, He stedfastly set His face to go to Jerusalem."[2] These words and actions all show how earnest and intense was His desire, promptly, and with no delay, to do the will of His Father in heaven. They suggest, also, how severe was the strain upon His patience, and how exemplary and praiseworthy was His submission during that larger portion of His earthly life which was shrouded in clouds and darkness. He served, by patient continuance in well-doing, in the position and under the circumstances in which He was placed. In this all may follow Him.

> "Law and prophets to fulfil,
> Was My life devoted still;
> For I came to do His will.
>
> What that will the Scripture saith;
> Thirty years of Nazareth,
> Three years' public work—then death."

[1] Luke ix. 28–31.   [2] Luke ix. 51.

III.

BAPTISM AND PRIESTHOOD.

CHAPTER III.

BAPTISM AND PRIESTHOOD.

CONNECTED with the baptism of Jesus is the strong preliminary testimony of John, the son of Zacharias and Elisabeth. His preaching and austere manner had attracted great multitudes. "And there went out unto him all the land of Judea, and they of Jerusalem, and were all baptized of him in the river of Jordan, confessing their sins." "And as the people were in expectation, and all men mused in their hearts of John, whether he were the Christ, or not; John answered, saying unto them all, I indeed baptize you with water; but one mightier than I cometh, the latchet of whose shoes I am not worthy to unloose: He shall baptize you with the Holy Ghost and with fire."[1] The meaning of John was, that this baptism would be unspeakably more efficacious than his own, in that the Christ would bestow the penetrating and searching power of the Holy Ghost. He may have had in mind the words of Malachi iii. 2, where the Messiah is compared to a "refiner's fire." John further testifies that not only His baptism but His authority will be greater, for He will bring all men before His tribunal, to be awarded according to their deeds. "Whose fan is in His hand, and He will throughly purge His floor, and will gather the wheat into His garner; but the chaff He will burn with fire unquenchable."[2] Whilst this was honourable testimony, it was also an argument, an intensely effective argument, to persuade men to repent. "Knowing therefore the terror of the Lord, we persuade men." "The Jews sent priests and Levites from Jerusalem to ask him, Who art thou?"[3] This question virtually was, Art thou the Christ? John "confessed, and denied not; but confessed, I am not the Christ." "Art

---

[1] Luke iii. 15, 16.   [2] Luke iii. 17.
[3] 2 Cor. v. 11; John i. 19.

thou Elias? And he saith, I am not. Art thou that Prophet?"—referring doubtless to the words of Moses,[1] "The Lord thy God will raise up unto thee a Prophet from the midst of thee, of thy brethren, like unto me; unto him ye shall hearken,"—"And he answered, No." Perplexed, but not satisfied, they earnestly said, "Who art thou?" "What sayest thou of thyself?" "I am the voice of one crying in the wilderness, Make straight the way of the Lord, as said the prophet Esaias." "The voice of him that crieth in the wilderness, Prepare ye the way of the Lord, make straight in the desert a highway for our God." As you desire an answer for those who sent you, tell them I am sent of God as the harbinger of the Messiah, whose character and office you will find described in the writings of the Prophet Isaiah.

As it is the business of the forerunner of the Messiah to lead the people to Him, so "the next day John seeth Jesus coming unto him, and saith, Behold the Lamb of God, which taketh away the sin of the world. This is He of whom I said, After me

[1] Deut. xviii. 15.

cometh a man which is preferred before me." "I knew Him not" when I first testified concerning the Messiah, that He was soon to appear. I then only knew that by my mission and baptism "He should be made manifest to Israel; therefore am I come baptizing with water." "But He that sent me to baptize with water, the same said unto me, Upon whom thou shalt see the Spirit descending, and remaining on Him, the same is He which baptizeth with the Holy Ghost." And "I saw the Spirit descending from heaven like a dove, and it abode upon Him," and I bare record that this is the Son of God. "Again the next day after John stood, and two of his disciples; and looking upon Jesus as He walked, he saith, Behold the Lamb of God!" John saw and declared Jesus to be the innocent, pure victim, the sacrificial Lamb chosen of God, "the Lamb slain from the foundation of the world." When the two disciples heard him thus speak, "they followed Jesus." The name of Andrew, the brother of Simon Peter, is given, whilst the characteristic modesty of the beloved disciple conceals his own. These were the first two who openly followed Christ, and who were numbered among the apostles.[1]

AT THE RIVER JORDAN.

By the law of Moses, it has already been stated, no priest could enter upon his public duties until he had reached the age of thirty.[2] That same law required a washing, or baptism, as the symbol of purification. "And Aaron and his sons thou shalt bring unto the door of the tabernacle of the congregation, and shalt wash them with water."[3] "And Moses brought Aaron and his sons, and washed them with water."[4] "And thus shalt thou do unto them, to cleanse them: Sprinkle water of purifying upon them."[5] There were among the Jews two kinds of baptism. One was that of the priests, as already stated. The other, which is not, however, expressly mentioned in Scripture, was that of the heathen

---

[1] In order to have the unbroken testimony of John, I have not strictly followed the order of history. Some of the utterances quoted were made prior to and some after the baptism of our Lord.

[2] See p. 40. [3] Exod. xxix. 4; xl. 12.
[4] Lev. viii. 6. [5] Num. viii. 7.

when proselytised to the true religion.[1] Being familiar with this usage, no objection was made to the baptisms by John. The messengers from the Sanhedrim asked, "Why baptizest thou then, if thou be not that Christ, nor Elias, neither that Prophet?" In this they asked for his authority, for it is said to have been a current opinion that all the Jews were to be baptized either by the Messiah or by some of His retinue. They thus understood the prophet,—" In that day there shall be a fountain opened to the house of David and to the inhabitants of Jerusalem for sin and for uncleanness."[2] This may account for the fact that such vast multitudes crowded to the baptism of John, which was the baptism of repentance.

Whilst John was at Bethabara, "the place of the ford,"—a town on the east bank of the river Jordan,—Jesus "came from Galilee unto John, to be baptized of him."[3] Conscious of his own inferiority, John was forbidding Him, "saying, I have need to be baptized of

---

[1] The existence of this practice in New Testament times has been questioned. I regard the evidence in its favour as sufficient, for reasons which cannot be discussed within the limits of the present work.

[2] Zech. xiii. 1.   [3] Matt. iii. 13.

Thee, and comest Thou to me?" The man who received confessions from others now makes confession to Jesus. Under a Divine impulse he recognised Jesus as the Messiah, and attempted to hinder Him. This conviction was afterwards confirmed to him by the visible descent of the Holy Spirit. "And Jesus answering said unto him, Suffer it to be so now: for thus it becometh us to fulfil all righteousness." This reply is the second recorded utterance of Jesus. It is not a confession of penitence, as He was sinless. He does not say, "I have the same need as others to be baptized," but, " Thus it becometh us to fulfil all righteousness." As the law demands the baptism of the priest, so now I, entering upon that office, submit to the requirement. "Think not that I am come to destroy the law and the prophets; I am not come to destroy, but to fulfil." The baptism of Christ being therefore an act of obedience to the letter and the spirit of the law, He urged it, and John no longer protesting, He was baptized, in the presence of a multitude of spectators. I enter not into the question of the mode, since that which all will admit was infinitely superior immediately occurred — the baptism of the Holy Ghost. "And Jesus, when He was baptized, went up straightway out of the water;" "and praying," "lo, the heavens were opened unto Him, and he [John] saw the Spirit of God descending like a dove, and lighting upon Him." This was a fit emblem of the gentle and peaceful character of Jesus and His mission. Luke says, "The Holy Ghost descended in a bodily shape like a dove upon Him." This may imply that a material symbol of the Spirit's presence had on this occasion the shape as well as the motion of a dove. Whether it is to be understood as referring to the *shape*, or to a dove-like radiance that hovered over him, or to the *manner* of a dove when alighting, are unsettled questions. On the day of Pentecost we read that "there appeared unto them cloven tongues, like as of fire, and it sat upon each of them, and they were all filled with the Holy Ghost." That on the entrance of Christ on His mission there was a special and marked manifestation of the Holy Ghost, is the all-important point. It is worthy of particular notice how continuously the Scriptures connect the Holy

Ghost with Christ personally. Of the Messiah it was predicted: "And there shall come forth a rod out of the stem of Jesse, and a Branch shall grow out of his roots; and the Spirit of the Lord shall rest upon Him."[1] "The Spirit of the Lord God is upon Me; because the Lord hath anointed Me to preach good tidings."[2] In the synagogue at Nazareth, Christ read this latter passage, and said, "This day is this Scripture fulfilled in your ears."[3] "And all bare Him witness, and wondered at the gracious words which proceeded out of His mouth." Immediately after the baptism it is written, "And Jesus being full of the Holy Ghost returned from Jordan, and was led by the Spirit into the wilderness." Again, "And Jesus returned in the power of the Spirit into Galilee." Still further, "After that He through the Holy Ghost had given commandments unto the apostles whom He had chosen."[4] When Peter preached to the household gathering of Cornelius, he declared "how God anointed Jesus of Nazareth with the Holy Ghost and with power."[5] Thus

[1] Isa. xi. 1, 2. [2] Isa. lxi. 1.
[3] Luke iv. 21. [4] Luke iv. 1, 14; Acts i. 2.
[5] Acts x. 38.

from the annunciation, "The Holy Ghost shall come upon thee, and the power of the Highest shall overshadow thee," until His whole earthly work was finished, our Lord, in His human nature, was filled with the Holy Ghost, and was always under His guidance and power. "Wherefore in all things it behoved Him to be made like unto His brethren." From His own experience, knowing the indwelling blessedness of the Holy Spirit, He promised to His disciples, through all time, the energising power of the Holy Ghost. "I will not leave you comfortless." "I will pray the Father, and He shall give you another Comforter, that He may abide with you for ever; even the Spirit of Truth." "The Comforter, which is the Holy Ghost, whom the Father will send in My name, He shall teach you all things." "He breathed on them, and saith unto them, Receive ye the Holy Ghost." On the day of Pentecost " they were all filled with the Holy Ghost." "Then Peter, filled with the Holy Ghost, spake before the rulers." The qualification of the seven deacons was that they were "full of the Holy Ghost." Of Stephen it is especially recorded that he was "a man full of faith and of the Holy Ghost." The churches "walking in the fear of the Lord and in the comfort of the Holy Ghost were multiplied." Barnabas "was a good man, and full of the Holy Ghost and of faith, and much people was added unto the Lord." At Antioch "the disciples were filled with joy and with the Holy Ghost."

The history of the church, as well as that of individual experience, teaches that only when they are "full of faith and of the Holy Ghost" they have joy and comfort, and are making progress in the Divine life, and successfully promoting the salvation of men. Being full of the Holy Ghost, they become like Christ. How appropriate for any Christian is the prayer of David: "Create in me a clean heart, O God; and renew a right spirit within me. Cast me not away from Thy presence; and take not Thy Holy Spirit from me. Restore unto me the joy of Thy salvation and uphold me with Thy free Spirit. Then will I teach transgressors Thy ways; and sinners shall be converted unto Thee."[1]

[1] Psa. li. 10–13.

When the heavens opened, and the Holy Ghost descended and lighted upon Jesus, "there came a voice from heaven, saying, This is My beloved Son, in whom I am well pleased." What was this voice? It was the voice of God the Father, loud and distinct;— not to be mistaken for thunder, or the speech of an angel, as it was on a subsequent occasion.[1] It was so loud and peculiar as to be unlike the sighing of the wind or the inquiring voices of the multitude. It was clear and articulate, so that all who heard understood the utterance: "This is My beloved Son, in whom I am well pleased." The Son of God was one of the titles of the Messiah, indicating His Divine nature. "The Lord Himself shall give you a sign: behold a virgin shall conceive and bear a son, and shall call His name Immanuel," "which, being interpreted, is, God with us;" "therefore that holy thing which shall be born of thee shall be called the Son of God." This testimony was repeated at the transfiguration, "This is My beloved Son, in whom I am well pleased; hear ye Him." And again in a modified form in Jerusalem, "Then came

[1] John xii. 29.

there a voice from heaven, saying, **I have both glorified it and will glorify it again.**" The High Priest said, "Art Thou the Christ, the Son of the Blessed? And Jesus said, I am." Then **they** charged Him with blasphemy. When Jesus claimed that God was His Father, "the Jews sought the more to kill Him, because He said that God was His Father, making Himself equal with God." He was "declared to be the Son of God with power, according to the Spirit of holiness, by the resurrection from the dead."

At the baptism of Jesus, there was the clear manifestation of the Holy Trinity. Not, as some have taught, three offices of God; not, as others have taught, three powers, such as are seen in man—mind and heart and will; but three distinct Persons: the **Father,** speaking from heaven; the Son, **standing in His incarnation on the bank of the river** Jordan; and the Holy Ghost, visibly lighting upon the Redeemer. This voice from heaven and this anointing with the Holy Ghost, are the grand distinguishing incidents **of** the baptism of **Christ.**

This was more than baptism. It was the holy anointing of Jesus as the great High

Priest. Predicted by the prophets of the old economy, He came, and was thus publicly, with special Divine honours, inaugurated as the Apostle and High Priest of the new dispensation: "The Lord hath sworn, and will not repent, Thou art a priest for ever after the order of Melchizedek."[1] "He shall bear the glory, and shall sit and rule upon His throne; and He shall be a priest upon His throne."[2] Prophecy declared that the priestly and the kingly offices should be united in Him; a union not found in any Levitical High Priest. Prophecy forbade that His priesthood should be of the Aaronic order. It declared that it should be after the peculiar and unique order of Melchizedek. This Melchizedek was "king of Salem and priest of the most high God."[3] His priesthood was not hereditary: "Without father, without mother, without descent, having neither beginning of days, nor end of life; but made like unto the Son of God; [he] abideth a priest continually." Thus emphatically is it stated that the priesthood of Melchizedek was unique and exceptional, that it had no

[1] Psa. cx. 4. [2] Zech. vi. 13. [3] Gen. xiv. 18; Heb. vii.

ancestry and no pedigree, that he neither received it from any ancestor nor transmitted it to any successor; that in this respect he symbolised the Son of God, whose priesthood is not received by birth, or tribe, or transmitted by death, as was the Levitical. Thus in Christ the law of the descent from Aaron is set aside, because He comes of an order more ancient and honourable than that of Levi.

The grand, distinctive, and glorious act of the priesthood of Jesus was the offering up of Himself as an atoning sacrifice, thus fulfilling and authenticating all the sacrifices by blood of the earlier dispensation. "I lay down My life for the sheep." "I lay down My life, that I might take it again. No man taketh it from Me, but I lay it down of Myself. I have power to lay it down, and I have power to take it again."[1] When He had finished the last passover, as the Priest of the new dispensation, He "took bread, and blessed it, and brake it, and gave it to the disciples, and said, Take, eat; this is My body. And He took the cup, and gave thanks,

[1] John x. 15, 17, 18.

and gave it to them, saying, Drink ye all of it; for this is My blood of the new testament, which is shed for many for the remission of sins."[1] "Whoso eateth My flesh, and drinketh My blood, hath eternal life; and I will raise him up at the last day."[2]

During His public ministry He gave proof of His priesthood as no Aaronic priest could possibly do. In His own name, and by His personal power, He forgave sin. "And, behold, men brought in a bed a man which was taken with a palsy. . . . When He saw their faith, He said unto him, Man, thy sins are forgiven thee. And the scribes and the Pharisees began to reason, saying, Who is this which speaketh blasphemies? Who can forgive sins, but God alone? But when Jesus perceived their thoughts," He gave ocular miraculous demonstration of His priestly power to forgive sin: "He answering said unto them, What reason ye in your hearts? Whether it is easier, to say, Thy sins be forgiven thee; or to say, Rise up and walk? But that ye may know that the Son of man hath power upon earth to forgive sins,

[1] Matt. xxvi. 26-28. [2] John vi. 54.

(He said unto the sick of the palsy,) I say unto thee, Arise, and take up thy couch, and go into thine house. And immediately he rose up before them, and took up that whereon he lay, and departed to his own house, glorifying God."[1]

The triumphant confidence which we may repose in Him is thus set forth, "He is able to save them to the uttermost that come unto God by Him, seeing He ever liveth to make intercession for them. For such an high priest became us, who is holy, harmless, undefiled, separate from sinners, and made higher than the heavens; who needeth not daily, as those high priests, to offer up sacrifice, first for His own sins, and then for the people's: for this He did once, when He offered up Himself. For the law maketh men high priests which have infirmity; but the word of the oath, which was since the law, maketh the Son, who is consecrated (perfected) for evermore." "We have such an high priest, who is set on the right hand of the throne of the Majesty in the heavens; a minister of the sanctuary, and of the true tabernacle, which the Lord

[1] Luke v. 18-25.

pitched, and not man." "But Christ being come an high priest of good things to come, by a greater and more perfect tabernacle, not made with hands, that is to say, not of this building; neither by the blood of goats and calves, but by His own blood He entered in once into the holy place, having obtained eternal redemption for us."

Thus harmonious is the revelation; the arguments of the apostle illustrating the record of the evangelist. The baptism of Jesus was no solitary fact in His history, nor did it rank with that of the multitudes who "were baptized by John in Jordan." There was a meaning in His submission to the ordinance —though John himself knew it not—impressive and unique. It was the response of the Son to the call of the Father. "Lo I come, to do Thy will, O God!" It was the earthly symbol, at the very commencement of His ministry, of His dedication to that office which, by self-sacrifice and heavenly intercession, He should carry on until He "shall see of the travail of His soul, and shall be satisfied." The Son, the only High Priest of the new covenant, is "consecrated for evermore."

IV.

THE TEMPTATION.

CHAPTER IV.

THE TEMPTATION.

THE facts of this momentous transaction are few, and are clearly stated. Still, there are connected with it deep and grave mysteries, which perhaps no finite mind can ever solve. As no disciples had yet been called, and as the record tells of no one accompanying Christ, it is evident that the narrative of the evangelists must have been communicated by the Lord. The statement by Mark is very brief, though comprehensive; whilst Matthew and Luke enter fully into details, agreeing as to all the facts, but differing as to the historic order of the temptations. We may not be able to apprehend all the considerations which account for and explain this scene in the wilderness. Some are obvious on the face of the record, and others are to be gathered from subsequent statements on the inspired page.

Mark says: " Immediately " (after His baptism) " the Spirit driveth Him into the wilderness." Matthew says: " He was led up of the Spirit into the wilderness." Luke says: " Jesus, being full of the Holy Ghost, was led by the Spirit into the wilderness." All agree that it was in obedience to a strong Divine impulse that our Lord went into the wilderness. Had He gone there only for devout meditation and prayer, preparatory to entering upon His public ministry, all would be plain; but when it is added, "to be tempted by the devil," anxious questions force themselves to the front. Why does the Holy Spirit lead Him to be tempted, when the Lord has taught us to pray, " Lead us not into temptation?" Why, when the Holy Ghost had descended upon Him with anointing power, is He subjected to so fearful and protracted an ordeal?

It was said to the serpent who deceived Eve, " I will put enmity between thee and the woman, and between thy seed and her seed ; it shall bruise thy head."[1] The time had come for this conflict, and Jesus, the seed of the woman, meets that "old serpent the devil," and vanquishes him, thus fulfilling the prediction, "It shall bruise thy head."

The true meaning of the word rendered "tempt" is, to try, or put to the proof. It does not necessarily imply an evil intention. When it is said, "God did tempt Abraham,"[2] it obviously means simply that God put his faith and obedience to proof or trial. The character of the temptation is always determined by the character of the being who brings the trial. God, being holy and good, tries His creatures, not to seduce them from virtue, but to prove them. Therefore it is written, "Let no man say when he is tempted, I am tempted of God: for God cannot be tempted with evil, neither tempteth He any man: but every man is tempted, when he is drawn away of his own lust, and enticed."[3] Here the word "tempt" is used in its bad sense, meaning to seduce to sin, and not in the sense of a trial of the character. Hence it is added, "Then when lust hath conceived, it bringeth

[1] Gen. iii. 15.   [2] Gen. xxii. 1.   [3] James i. 13, 14.

forth sin: and sin, when it is finished, bringeth forth death." But Satan, being unholy and malignant, **tempts men with** an evil purpose and design. God placed our first parents under the prohibition of the fruit of a single tree, to try their obedience. Satan came into the garden, and tempted them to disobedience and sin. The Holy Spirit led Jesus into the wilderness to be tried or proved. Satan came there to tempt, to seduce, him to sin.

This scene in the wilderness was not Christ's first temptation. As the Lord, in His human nature, had all the appetites and sources of temptation, bodily and mental, as other men, He was constantly tempted through youth and manhood, up to the time of His baptism. He was tempted by subjection to authority, by poverty, by the vicissitudes of labour, by ridicule, by the rebukes which His purity gave to others, by the maligning of His motives, by acts of unkindness, and numberless other ways by which the tempter sought to betray Him into unholy anger, or hasty utterances, or murmuring discontent, or in some way to betray Him into sin. The eye of the tempter was never removed from Him. From the attempt on His life through Herod, every step, every act, every moment, was watched with intensest interest, if, by any means, the devil could entangle Him in his meshes. Through all these years, the great majority of His life, He baffled all the wiles of the adversary.

In the trial in the wilderness some things are clearly illustrated.

1. As Jesus was tempted in the same line more severely and more extensively than was Adam, it demonstrates that there was no necessity for Adam, created "in the image of God," intelligent and holy, to sin. It proves that, as a free moral agent, he had the power to obey or disobey; and in his disobedience his sin was voluntary and inexcusable.

2. His example of successful resistance to temptation should be a strong encouragement to all His followers to stand firm against all the assaults of the adversary. The Captain of our salvation being made perfect (complete) "through sufferings," [1] and having Himself undergone all the hardships of His

[1] Heb. ii. 10.

service, no follower could complain of the trials to which he is subjected, as these trials are disciplinary and strengthening, and are far less than those Christ endured. Christ having endured poverty and reproach, the assaults of sensual pleasure, and every variety of temptation, His disciples may not only expect the same, but, through His grace, may hope to conquer.

3. He was tempted, that He might become a true and merciful High Priest. " Wherefore in all things it behoved Him to be made like unto His brethren, that He might be a merciful and faithful high priest in things pertaining to God, to make reconciliation for the sins of the people. For in that He Himself hath suffered, being tempted, He is able to succour them that are tempted."[1] "For we have not an high priest which cannot be touched with the feeling of our infirmities ; but was in all points tempted like as we are, yet without sin."[2] "God is faithful, who will not suffer you to be tempted above that ye are able ; but will with the temptation also make a way to escape, that ye may be able

[1] Heb. ii. 17, 18. [2] Heb. iv. 15.

to bear it."[1] "My grace is sufficient for thee: for My strength is made perfect in weakness."[2]

Temptation, if resisted, does no man any harm. Nay, it does him positive good. It strengthens right principles, and elevates him to a higher plane of moral excellence. "My brethren, count it all joy when ye fall into divers temptations" (trials, proofs); "knowing this, that the trying of your faith worketh patience. But let patience have her perfect work, that ye may be perfect and entire, wanting nothing. . . . Blessed is the man that endureth temptation: for when he is tried, he shall receive the crown of life, which the Lord hath promised to them that love Him."[3] "Be of good cheer; I have overcome the world."[4]

Temptation or trial is a necessity for all free, moral, and accountable beings, in order to develop and determine their character. The angels were put on probation. Some rebelled, and developed a permanent evil character. Those who stood

[1] 1 Cor. x. 13. [2] 2 Cor. xii. 9.
[3] James i. 2-4, 12. [4] John xvi. 33.

firm attained and maintained a higher permanent character of holiness.

The power to obey carries with it the power to disobey. As the Lord Jesus had a perfect human nature in all its bodily, mental, and moral faculties, He was subject, as were other men, to the laws of man's corporeal, mental, and moral nature.

Our Lord's human soul, though free from any tendency to evil, still was accessible to temptation from without. Whilst He could say "the prince of this world cometh, and hath nothing in Me," the tempter did come and plied his arts with persevering determination. Though tempted, and capable in His human nature of disobeying, He went through His ordeal without sin. It was morally certain that He would not sin. It is one thing to be tempted, and another to fall. "Though He were a Son, yet learned He obedience by the things which He suffered; and being made perfect, He became the author of eternal salvation unto all them that obey Him."

[1] Heb. v. 8, 9.

THE WILDERNESS.

The place of the temptation was "the wilderness." Mark adds, He "was with the wild beasts." It is not a matter of importance accurately to know the precise location of this wilderness. Some have supposed, from the brief description given of the scene, and from the quotations by our Lord from the Book of Deuteronomy,[1] that the wilderness was that in which Israel had wandered for forty years—some part of the great Sinaitic desert; but the prevailing opinion is that the place was not far from the eastern bank of the Jordan, and near the Dead Sea. Maundrell, in his Travels, thus describes this region: "It is a miserable and horrid place, consisting of high barren mountains, so that it looks as if nature had suffered some violent convulsions there." Into this desolate region Jesus entered alone. He had no social influence or support. Here He abode, "being forty days tempted of the devil." Of the nature of these temptations thus pertinaciously continued we have no record. They

---

[1] Deut. viii. 3; vi. 16; vi. 13; the three Scripture passages by which the three assaults of the tempter were repelled.

were such doubtless as were deeply felt by our Lord. "For," says Luther, "unless the tempting impression be felt, there is no real temptation." Though we cannot form any idea of the kind and variety of these long-continued trials, we can, with adoring gratitude, cherish the fact that in no one instance did the tempter gain the advantage. Jesus, with invincible resolution, stood firm. He grappled with the powers of the invisible world, and was the sinless victor. For, unless the temptation is acquiesced in, or yielded to, there is no sin.

THE FAST.

"When He had fasted forty days." "In those days He did eat nothing." Of Moses we read that on two occasions he fasted forty days and forty nights. The former was when he received the Law on Sinai. "I was gone up into the mount to receive the tables of stone, even the tables of the covenant which the Lord made with you, then I abode in the mount forty days and forty nights, I neither did eat bread nor drink water."[1] The latter occasion was when he interceded for

[1] Deut. ix. 9.

Israel, when they rebelled against the commandment of the Lord: "I fell down before the Lord forty days and forty nights, as I fell down at the first; because the Lord said He would destroy you."[1] "And I stayed in the mount, according to the first time, forty days and forty nights; and the Lord hearkened unto me at that time."[2] Thus, as the promulgator of the law, and the prevailing intercessor for his people, he was eminently the type of Christ.

We also read that Elijah, who was the type of Christ's forerunner, "arose, and did eat and drink, and went in the strength of that meat forty days and forty nights."[3] In these cases the miraculous power of God was exercised to keep His servants alive. Of our Lord it is said, "He did eat nothing." When persons are under high excitement they are, during the continuance of that excitement, hardly conscious of the cravings of hunger. Whether the mind thus excited so acts upon the stomach as, for the time being, to suspend its operations, or the mind is so intensified as to be unconscious of the pains of

[1] Deut. ix. 25.   [2] Deut. x. 10.   [3] 1 Kings xix. 8.

hunger, we know not. But of this there is no doubt : such a state of things, according to the laws of our being, could only continue for a very limited time. The long fast of our Lord can only be accounted for by the miraculous interposition, not of His own Divine power, but that of His Father. This does not militate against the fact that Christ, during His earthly abode, wrought no miracle for His own personal comfort.

THE TEMPTER.

As the time of trial drew to a close, the tempter comes more into the foreground. Various have been the theories advocated in relation to this whole transaction, and especially as to the appearance of Satan. Some maintain that there was no personal appearance, and that the narrative is only that of a vision. Kitto, in his Cyclopædia, remarks "that the accounts given by the evangelists convey no intimation that they refer to a vision ; that the feeling of hunger could not have been ideal; that a vision of forty days' continuance is incredible; that Moses, who was a type of Christ, saw no vision, and that hence it may be concluded Christ did not; that it is highly probable there would be a personal conflict between Christ and Satan when the former entered upon His ministry." We learn from Jude that Michael the archangel contended with the devil. This was personal, and not a vision. To cast himself down, in a vision, from the pinnacle of the Temple could have been no temptation, and could have no influence upon those in the courts below. The most probable opinion, we think, is, that a living personal devil did appear, and made his assaults upon our Lord.

This, we believe, is the legitimate teaching of the Scriptures. They represent Satan as a fallen spirit, perhaps an archangel, ruined: a being of immense mental force and activity, and of deep, settled, determined malignity. To him they ascribe great control; subordinating natural agencies to his service: "The prince of the power of the air."[1] "The prince of this world."[2] They call him "Beelzebub, the prince of the devils."[3] "The chief of the devils."[4] Being their

---

[1] Ephes. ii. 2.   [2] John xii. 31.
[3] Matt. xii. 24.   [4] Luke xi. 15.

leader, he controls an immense number of other fallen spirits, who are obedient to his will. He is not omnipresent, but he stations in every part of the world these, his faithful servants, so that they may study human nature in all its various phases, and adapt their temptations accordingly, and thus carry out his malign purposes. His existence is recognised, not in one book and by one writer only of the Scriptures, but by many writers, who lived in different countries, and under diverse circumstances and at distant periods from each other. "Every quality, every action which can indicate personality, is attributed to him in language which cannot be explained away." The inspired writers give to him names and titles which appropriately belong only to a person, a living responsible being. The character which they assign to him can only belong to a person. "The devil sinneth from the beginning."[1] "He was a murderer from the beginning, and abode not in the truth, because there is no truth in him. When he speaketh a lie, he speaketh of his own: for he is a liar, and the father of it."[2]

[1] John iii. 8.   [2] John viii. 44.

HIS AGENCY.

He has great knowledge of human nature, which he has studied for thousands of years, under all its possible varieties. He thus has the power of knowing every man's weak point, whether of lust, or avarice, or pleasure, or pride. He presents to human appetites and passions their special objects in such vivid and captivating forms as to excite them, and, through them, to get the consent of the will. "Every man is tempted, when he is drawn away of his own lust, and enticed. Then when lust hath conceived, it bringeth forth sin: and sin, when it is finished, bringeth forth death."[1] The methods he uses are called fiery darts, depths, devices, wiles, and a deceivableness of unrighteousness. At times he comes "like a roaring lion, seeking whom he may devour," thus appealing to the fears of men. But oftener his approaches are more quiet, stealthy, and seductive. His presence is not suspected, and his wiles are not detected until the victim falls into "the snare of the devil," and is "taken captive by him at his will."[2]

---
[1] James i. 14, 15.
[2] 2 Tim. ii. 26; according to the ordinary interpretation.

"I fear, lest by any means, as the serpent beguiled Eve through his subtilty, so your minds should be corrupted from the simplicity that is in Christ. . . . And no marvel; for Satan himself is transformed into an angel of light."[1]

Satanic influence is spoken of in the Scriptures in the strongest terms as a reality, to continue until the final judgment.

The question most practical, and of deepest concern to us, is this: Has Satan direct access to the human mind? From the way in which some Christians speak, — "The devil put that into my mind;" "I was led by the devil;" "Satan controlled me;" "Satan has entered into me;"—they seem to throw the blame for their evil thoughts, and consequent actions, on Satan, and at least evade the acknowledgment of their own sin. This is neither fair nor safe. Some passages, no doubt, appear to favour the theory that Satan has direct access to the mind, and can either produce evil thoughts and decisions or prevent the good. It is written, "Then cometh the wicked one, and catcheth away that which

[1] 2 Cor. xi. 3, 14.

was sown in his heart."[1] "Then entered Satan into Judas surnamed Iscariot." "After the sop Satan entered into him."[2] But Christ had previously said, "Have not I chosen you twelve, and one of you is a devil?"[3] Christ knew that the heart of Judas was evil, and in sympathy with Satan. "An evil man out of the evil treasure bringeth forth evil things."[4] "For out of the heart of men proceed evil thoughts, adulteries, fornications, murders, thefts, covetousness, wickedness, deceit, lasciviousness, an evil eye, blasphemy, pride, foolishness; all these evil things come from within."[5] The passages which seem to teach that Satan has direct access to the mind, and may originate wicked devices, must be so understood as to harmonise with other passages which show that he approaches and operates through external instrumentalities. Satan understood Judas well. He knew his revengeful temper and the avarice of his heart, and plied these with the temptation suited to the man and the occasion; thus, it may be said, entering into him. He de-

---

[1] Matt. xiii. 19.   [2] Luke xxii. 3; John xiii. 27.
[3] John vi. 70.   [4] Matt. xii. 35.   [5] Mark vii. 21-23.

sired to have Peter, that he might sift him "as wheat." But the Lord said, "I have prayed for thee, that thy faith fail not."[1] Judas was left to the workings of his own evil heart, and Satan had power over him. But Peter was guarded, and was held by the prayers of his Lord.

MENTAL LAWS.

There are laws of the mind, not clearly understood by all, which may explain what many regard as direct satanic suggestions.

When in the closet praying, a single word may, by the law of association, arouse the memory of wicked words uttered or heard in days of impenitence, but which now agitate the soul and destroy its peace. You find that when again praying, at the set period, the same evil suggestions recur. This same law associates them with this place and time. Change the place and the time, and you break the force of this law. Your pastor, on the Sabbath, quotes a text, and this law of association brings to mind some ribald use made of this passage by an evil companion, whose

[1] Luke xxii. 31, 32.

wit you once laughed at; but now it troubles you. Some object strikes your eye, whilst walking and devoutly meditating; it quickens into life some long-forgotten evil practice and overwhelms you with desperate memories. It was not necessarily Satan, but only the law of association, ever active, which thus filled your mind so inopportunely with troublesome evil thoughts. If these are instantly resisted and repelled, they do you no harm; but if ever so slightly cherished, they leave the stain of sin.

Imagination is a power through which Satan acts with great success. Through evil-minded men he has subordinated the fine arts,—statuary, painting, and music,—as well as literature, in some of its most refined as well as its grosser forms, to his own purposes. Fashions in female attire have been, and in some quarters still are, another potent agency. He so uses all these and similar things, that through the imagination he fires the passions, and seduces into sinful thoughts and desires, if not to guilty conduct.

Even in the conduct of religious services,

by scenic representations, splendid robes, and captivating forms, through the imagination emotions are awakened which the unwary mistake for religion, whilst there is no penitence for and forsaking of sin; no sense of guilt and need of pardon; no true spiritual worship. Thus he deludes multitudes with the assurance that they are truly pious.

Curiosity is also a power by which Satan leads men on step by step from that which is proper to that which excites and inflames the passions and pollutes, until the barriers of virtue are broken down, and by "giving heed to seducing spirits, and doctrines of demons" the unwary are ruined.[1]

We know that one bad man has a strange influence over others. This influence is felt when not a word is spoken. A look will excite. But without a look it is felt. Simply his presence does the work. There is a sympathy of evil. So Satan has this power in a greater degree of awakening sympathetic thought. For there is evil in every heart, evil to which he can appeal. " Keep thy

---

[1] Is there not an explanation here of much which in modern times goes by the name of "spiritualism"?

heart with all diligence; for out of it are the issues of life."

There are no intimations in the Bible that the holy angels, who rejoice over the repentance of sinners, and who are ministering spirits to the heirs of salvation, have direct access to the mind, or that they suggest good thoughts. We know that it is the Holy Spirit who thus acts. If God has not given direct access to the mind to the good angels, much less would he give it to malignant beings bent upon the ruin of souls. This prerogative belongs only to the Omniscient One. "I the Lord search the heart, I try the reins."[1] "The Lord looketh on the heart."[2] "The Lord searcheth all hearts, and understandeth all the imaginations of the thoughts."[3] "I am He which searcheth the reins and hearts."[4]

The question about demoniacal possession I do not here discuss, as this was a peculiarity of that day. Then, as Christ had come to destroy the works of the devil, Satan seems to have been permitted to manifest

---

[1] Jer. xvii. 10.
[2] 1 Sam. xvi. 7.
[3] 1 Chron. xxviii. 9.
[4] Rev. ii. 23.

his wrath, and to afflict the bodies of men in addition to his usual methods.

OLD TESTAMENT INSTANCES.

A careful examination of the typical Old Testament cases of satanic temptation will demonstrate that the tempter reaches the mind from without, through the animal appetites and mental aspirations.

In the case of our first parents, we are told that, "When the woman saw that the tree was good for food [lust of the flesh], and that it was pleasant to the eyes [the lust of the eyes], and a tree to be desired to make one wise [the pride of life], she took of the fruit thereof, and did eat, and gave also unto her husband with her, and he did eat."[1] The temptation was from without. It was through the senses that he reached her mind. "The woman said, The serpent beguiled me." The inspired comment is, "Adam was not deceived, but the woman being deceived was in the transgression."[2]

In the temptation of the patriarch Job, so varied and continued, it is especially remark-

[1] Gen. iii. 6.   [2] 1 Tim. ii. 14.

able that no evidence of direct spiritual action upon the mind is attributed to Satan. To him were permitted extraordinary powers, even to personal afflictions; still, his whole work on Job, so far as the record goes, was from without. Through outward circumstances he strove to break down the faith and "endurance" of the patriarch, and so to prove that his religion was mercenary.

It can scarcely be doubted that as with our first parents and with Job, so with Jesus, the tempter made the senses the medium of assault. It is quite true that there is a mystery here, arising from Christ's Divine personality. Satan, before his rebellion, and when loyal, must have had knowledge of the Son, the second Person of the sacred Trinity, and worshipped Him. He would also know from the Scriptures that the Son was to become incarnate, and, as the Messiah, to introduce the redemptive scheme. He would know, from the prophecies and the peculiar facts attending the birth of Jesus, that the predicted time of deliverance had come.

Yet his malignant nature inspired him with the desperate purpose of seducing Him, by appeals to His human appetites and aspirations into one sin—only one. For this would prevent the making of an atonement, and would secure the ruin of all men. He had ruined the first Adam by his appeal to the "lust of the flesh," the "lust of the eyes," and the "pride of life." So he hoped also to prevail with the second Adam.

THE FIRST TRIAL.

The temptation of Christ was eminently a representative instance. Not that His and our temptations are the same. Far from it. Satan found in Him not only a sinless being, but one having no tendency to sin; while we are actual sinners, with an evil heart. But His trial shows from whence is our danger: for, as his assaults were from without, and directed to His bodily appetite and pains, so these are the avenues through which Satan will try to seduce us to sin. Thus are we forewarned, and admonished most vigilantly to guard these gates of entrance, "lest Satan should get an advantage of us; for we are not ignorant of his devices."

" He was afterward an hungred;" "He

afterward hungred." The tempter understood the situation, and vainly thought himself to be the master of the occasion. "He said unto Him, If thou be the Son of God, command that these stones be made bread." "The angel in the annunciation said that Thou shouldest 'be called the Son of God.' John the Baptist has pointed Thee out as 'The Lamb of God.' And at Thy baptism the voice from heaven said, ' My beloved Son.' Now is a fit occasion to settle all doubts. If indeed Thou art the Son of God, prove Thy Divinity by this miracle: 'command that these stones be made bread,' and at once supply the wants of Thy nature, exhausted by so long a fast." Specious and seductive reasoning! But the Lord understood that a compliance would be an act of unbelief and want of confidence in His Father, who had sustained His animal life during the long fast in which "He ate nothing." He appealed to the Scriptures as the only infallible guide, and said, "It is written, man shall not live by bread alone, but by every word that proceedeth out of the mouth of God." Jesus believed the truth, and was resolute in His trust in God, and thus rejected the temptation.

THE SECOND TRIAL.

Having failed in his first attempt, with persevering malignity Satan tries another expedient. "Then the devil taketh Him up into the holy city." There are various theories as to the method by which the tempter accomplished this. Some make it a flight through the air. Benson, in his *Life of Christ*, and Doddridge, in his *Harmony*, say, "The devil took our Lord about with him as one person takes another to different places. 'Taketh Him along with him' is the exact English of the Greek." They suppose that Satan appeared in a human form, and personated an honest inquirer for the truth, desiring to have proof that He was the Messiah. Archbishop Secker says, "Certainly he did not appear what he was, for that would have frustrated his intent." Chandler also says: "The devil appeared not as himself, for that would have frustrated the effect of his temptation." He thinks he appeared "as a good man."

Whatever was his appearance, and how he accomplished the transit to Jerusalem, the fact remains; it was for the purpose of a specific temptation: "And setteth Him on a pinnacle of the temple," rather, "on the battlement." As in Palestine the roofs of the houses were flat, the law required "thou shalt make a battlement for thy roof, that thou bring not blood upon thine house, if any man fall from thence."[1] The Temple proper, called Naos, in which were the Holy Place and the Holy of Holies, was a comparatively small building; but around were massive and lofty cloisters, with battlements on the outer edges of the roofs. It was on one of these that Jesus stood, probably on that around the men's court, in which great numbers of the Jews daily assembled. The place and time were well chosen for a demonstration of the Divine power. "And saith unto Him, If Thou be the Son of God, cast Thyself down." "Look below: there the multitude are anxiously discussing the prophecies concerning the Messiah, and wondering whether this Jesus of Nazareth is the promised One. Solve all

[1] Deut. xxii. 8.

their doubts by this one act : 'Cast Thyself down.'" Here is an appeal, not so much to the lower appetites, as to the nobler elements of our nature. " Cast Thyself down." "Do not hesitate, for there can be no possible personal danger ; 'For it is written, He shall give His angels charge concerning Thee [over Thee, to keep Thee], and in their hands they shall bear Thee up, lest at any time Thou dash Thy foot against a stone.' Now prove Thyself to be the Son of God. When from this height Thou lightest unharmed upon the pavement below, they will see that Thou art under the special care of God. They will with one accord acknowledge that Thou comest with a Divine commission. The work of convincing the rulers will be ended, and they will announce Thee as their expected Messiah. 'Cast Thyself down,' therefore, for the angels are vigilant and at hand." To this urgent, special pleading, "Jesus said unto him, It is written again, Thou shalt not tempt the Lord thy God." Says Canon Farrar : " Thou shalt not, as it were, presume on all that He can do for Thee ; Thou shalt not claim His miraculous intervention to save

Thee from Thine own presumption and folly; Thou shalt not challenge His power to the proof." Had the devil, with power superior to mere human strength, cast Him over the battlement, such an appeal would have involved no presumption on the part of Christ, and God might then properly, by ministering angels or otherwise, interpose for His safety. In such a case, the tempter knew, there would be no sin. "Jesus said unto him, It is written again, Thou shalt not tempt the Lord thy God." The immediate application, doubtless, was to Himself as forbidding Him to comply with the temptation. But perhaps, also, personal application to the devil is admissible. As though Christ had said, " You professedly desire proof that I am the Son of God; I tell you that I am, and it is forbidden in the same scriptures to 'tempt the Lord thy God.'"

THE THIRD TRIAL.

Though thwarted and sternly rebuked, Satan does not give up. His determination is invigorated by his malignant hatred. Like the desperate gambler, he resolves to stake all upon a last throw. He gathers up all his forces, and offers a splendid bribe for one, only one act,—the reverential acknowledgment of his authority. He makes his appeal to ambition, the love of power and distinction, to the pleasures and gratification which extended rule and authority give. With only one of these seductions he had bound many millions. Who can stand before their united force? "He taketh Him up into an exceeding high mountain,[1] and showeth Him all the

[1] "What mountain this was," says the Annotated Paragraph Bible, "cannot be determined. From many elevations the kingdoms, or tetrarchies, of Palestine could be seen at once. The more distant regions, and empires of the world, might be suggested by the tempter." The original Greek word for "show" means "to make known, to declare, to announce," as in Matt. xvi. 21: "From that time forth began Jesus to show unto His disciples, how that He must go unto Jerusalem, and suffer many things of the elders and chief priests," etc. Here "show" is, to make known, to declare, not by vision or by actual sight, but by His word. With the same use of the Greek word which our Lord employed when foretelling to His disciples the events which would occur when He should enter Jerusalem, we may understand that the devil *declared* to Him that all the kingdoms of the world, with their glory, he would give to Him for one single act of homage. It is as though he said, "I am the acknowledged god of this world, for it has been given unto me. Now, the whole I will give and surrender to Thy absolute control, on the easy condition of one act of homage." This interpretation relieves the passage of the difficulty of seeming to suggest the geographical impossibility of seeing all the kingdoms of the world from any mountain elevation. Some of the Greek poets have the same use of the original word.

kingdoms of this world, and the glory of them; and saith unto Him, All these things will I give Thee, if Thou wilt fall down and worship me." Stop, bold usurper! These are *not thine!* When you were a bright, loyal spirit before the throne, you knew that "the Word was with God, and the Word was God," that "all things were made by Him; and without Him was not any thing made that was made;"[1] "For by Him were all things created, that are in heaven, and that are in earth, visible and invisible, whether they be thrones, or dominions, or principalities, or powers: all things were created by Him, and for Him."[2] Creation is the highest possible proof of ownership. Christ has never parted with His right. How unblushing is the impudent effrontery of the devil! He promises to give unto Christ that which already belongs to Him, and asks in return the homage which is due to no creature, but to God only. Driven from this claim of original ownership, he says: "'It is delivered unto me, and to whomsoever I will I give it,' for I am 'the god of

---

[1] John i. 1, 3.   [2] Col. i. 16.

this world.' As such I make this offer. I know that Thou art the Messiah, the Son of God, and that ultimately Thou wilt triumph and possess all. But I am in possession, and it will be long years of desperate conflict before the victory is gained. All I ask is to treat me as a sovereign, and make me but one act of reverential obeisance —just one act of worship. With that I will be content, and will retire, and give Thee and Thine no more trouble."—Whatever may have been the guise the tempter had assumed, the insulted Jesus stripped it off and revealed his true character. " Then saith Jesus unto him, Get thee hence, Satan." " Get thee behind Me, Satan." " Satan"— then He spoke to a person, not to an imagination, not to a vision. " Get thee hence, Satan, for it is written, Thou shalt worship the Lord thy God, and Him only shalt thou serve."[1] How exactly correspondent were the temptations of the first and of the second Adam! In each the appeal was to "the lust of the flesh, the lust of the eyes, and the pride of life." These had power with our first

---

[1] Deut. vi. 13.

parents, but failed utterly and signally with Christ. Such, as the apostle John teaches, are the sources of temptation in all the ages.[1] "And when the devil had ended all the temptation, he departed from Him for a season." Not for any long season, for His life was one continued temptation. The tempter was always present, with his diversified agencies. Follow up our blessed Lord, and you will know how He was tempted by the scribes and Pharisees and Herodians, in the almost countless methods by which they tried to entrap Him in His speech and conduct. He was tempted, sorely tempted, in the betrayal by one of His disciples, the denying Him by another, the forsaking Him by all. "The Prince of this world," He said, "is come!" Jesus was tempted by His seizure in the garden, by His examination before Annas, and by His unjust smiting there. He was tempted before Caiaphas and the Sanhedrim, when they "spit in His face, and buffeted Him, and blindfolded Him, and smote Him." He was tempted before Pilate, when the chief priests falsely accused Him. He was

[1] 1 John ii. 16.

tempted before Herod, who, with his men of war, set Him at nought and mocked, arraying Him in a gorgeous robe. He was tempted when His own nation rejected Him and chose Barabbas; when the whole band stripped Him, and, in mock royalty, clothed Him with purple, with a wreath of thorns for a crown, and a reed for a sceptre; when they smote and spit upon him;—tempted when Pilate scourged Him, and delivered Him, though innocent, to be crucified. These, all these, were trials—nay, every one a trial intensely severe. Yet He bore them all, and never, in action, word, or thought, sinned. From His birth to His death the tempter had Him under vigilant survey, and never lost an opportunity. Glorious Victor! through this whole life of temptation Thou wast tempted as no man ever was, yet without sin; and Thou hast sympathy for Thy tempted ones.

There remains one beautiful incident. "Angels came and ministered unto Him." They brought Him what He then most needed. This was food to nourish His body and strengthen Him after His long fast and sore ordeal. The Greek word is the same with that which expresses the office of a deacon. These angels brought food and served at table. Well might the Psalmist sing, "The Lord is my shepherd: I shall not want;" "Thou preparest a table before me in the presence of mine enemies."

WARNING AND HOPE.

The Scriptures abound in the most urgent warnings against the devices of the adversary. Yet, whilst they tell us that he is a mighty and skilful adversary, they comfort us with the assurance that he is not invincible. The example of Christ's temptations cheers us with the hope that, as His assaults were from without, we may, by prayerful watchfulness, escape the snares of the devil, and he get no advantage of us. The assurance is, "Resist the devil, and he will flee from you."[1] "Be sober, be vigilant; because your adversary the devil, as a roaring lion, walketh about, seeking whom he may devour: whom resist stedfast in the faith."[2] "Neither give place to the devil."[3] The apostle exhorts, "Be

[1] James iv. 7.   [2] 1 Peter v. 8, 9.   [3] Ephes. iv. 27.

strong in the Lord, and in the power of His might." To this end he says, " Put on the whole armour of God, that ye may be able to stand against the wiles of the devil." Why is this Divine panoply needed? Because " we wrestle not against flesh and blood, but against principalities, against powers, against the rulers of the darkness of this world, against spiritual wickedness in high places." Such being the vantage ground of the adversary, Paul renews his urgency : " Wherefore take unto you the whole armour of God, that ye may be able to withstand in the evil day; and, having done all, to stand." He illustrates his meaning by giving a spiritual turn to the Roman defensive armour: " Stand, therefore, having your loins girt about with truth, and having on the breastplate of righteousness; and your feet shod with the preparation of the gospel of peace ; above [or over] all, taking the shield of faith, wherewith ye shall be able to quench all the fiery darts of the wicked ; and take the helmet of salvation, and the sword of the Spirit, which is the Word of God." With all this panoply covering the body we are not safe, if we rely upon our own strength. Hence it is added, "Praying always with all prayer and supplication in the Spirit, and watching thereunto with all perseverance."[1] So taught our Lord, "Watch and pray, that ye enter not into temptation."[2] If we watch and do not pray, the tempter will prevail. If we pray and do not watch, the adversary will find an entrance. But if we both pray and watch, then our souls are guarded as by the cherubim at the garden of Eden, with a flaming sword, which turned every way. It is worthy of particular notice that all the armour is defensive, to repel assaults from without; and that the command is, "Having done all, to stand," facing the foe. There was no armour for the back. If we turn from facing the adversary, or attempt to flee, we are exposed to his fiery darts, with no shield to receive and quench them. Courage is indispensable. "Having done all, to stand."

The truth—the revealed truth of God—is the only infallible and invincible weapon. It was with this the Lord repelled the assaults of and vanquished the tempter, the

[1] Ephes. vi. 13–18.   [2] Matt. xxvi. 41.

father of lies. "For the word of God is quick and powerful, and sharper than any two-edged sword, piercing even to the dividing asunder of soul and spirit, and of the joints and marrow, and is a discerner of the thoughts and intents of the heart."[1] The prophet, when he spake God's words, said, "He hath made my mouth like a sharp sword." The apostle said, "The weapons of our warfare are not carnal." Because they are not carnal, but spiritual, they have life and power; are "mighty through God to the pulling down of strongholds;" "casting down imaginations, and every high thing that exalteth itself against the knowledge of God, and bringing into captivity every thought to the obedience of Christ."[2] Thus, with watchfulness and prayer, with faith and courage, and the word of Christ dwelling in us richly, we shall be kept from falling, and an entrance shall be ministered unto us abundantly into the everlasting kingdom of our Lord and Saviour Jesus Christ.

[1] Heb. iv. 12.   [2] 2 Cor. x. 4, 5.

V.

THE TRANSFIGURATION.

CHAPTER V.

THE TRANSFIGURATION.

MOUNTAINS stand out prominently in the Scriptures as the places where important events have occurred. Abraham was to offer Isaac for a burnt offering upon one of the mountains of Moriah. The law was proclaimed from Sinai. Moses died upon Nebo. It was upon Mount Carmel that fire came down from heaven—consumed the offering, the stones of the altar, "and licked up the water that was in the trench."[1] It was upon "an exceeding high mountain" that Christ was tempted of the devil. And now upon a "high mountain" the transfiguration, the most wonderful manifestation of the Divine glory

[1] 1 Kings xviii. 38.

in Christ, took place. Tradition for centuries fixed upon Mount Tabor as the sacred elevation. More careful examination of the narrative, with its connections, makes it plain that Tabor could not have been the mountain. The probabilities strongly settle upon Mount Hermon, which has an elevation of about ten thousand feet, and perfectly meets the designation "high mountain," while the transfiguration itself justifies the apostle Peter in calling it "the holy mountain."

"He took Peter and John and James, and went up into a mountain to pray."[1] It was, probably, in the early evening that He ascended. Only three of His disciples accompanied Him. Two of these He had called "sons of thunder," and the third "the man of rock." The avowed purpose of this seclusion was to pray. This was the habit of our Lord. "And when He had sent the multitudes away, He went up into a mountain apart to pray."[2] "And it came to pass in those days, that He went out into a mountain to pray, and continued all night in prayer."[3]

[1] Luke ix. 28.   [2] Matt. xiv. 23.   [3] Luke vi. 12.

The Transfiguration.

> "Night is the time to pray:
> The Saviour oft withdrew
> To distant mountains far away;
> So should His followers do:—
> Steal from the throng to haunts untrod,
> And hold communion there with God."

"As He prayed, the fashion of His countenance was altered,"[1] He "was transfigured before them: and His face did shine as the sun."[2] He was transformed, not in shape, but in the glory of His appearance. The word implies that a transformation took place in the substance of His body. This the apostle intimates: "Who shall change our vile body, that it may be fashioned like unto His glorious body."[3] "It doth not yet appear what we shall be: but we know that, when He shall appear, we shall be like Him."[4] "And His raiment was white and glistering;"[5] "was white as the light;"[6] "exceeding white as snow; so as no fuller on earth can white them."[7] He was "enwrapped in an aureole of glistering brilliance." The brightness which radiated from His person and garments is described by the most intense comparisons

[1] Luke ix. 29.   [2] Matt. xvii. 2.   [3] Phil. iii. 21.
[4] 1 John iii. 2.   [5] Luke ix. 29.   [6] Matt. xvii 2.
[7] Mark ix. 3.

known to men. But that glory of His Divinity, which transcended all these intensely brilliant demonstrations, could not be described.

"And, behold, there talked with Him two men, which were Moses and Elias: who appeared in glory, and spake of His decease which He should accomplish at Jerusalem."[1] They were two men, not angels, who now appeared. The one was Moses, the giver of the law and founder of the Jewish polity, and of supreme authority among the people of Israel. The other was Elijah, the most zealous reformer and prophet of the Jewish Church. Their presence at this time clearly attested that the ministry of Christ was the fulfilment of the law and the prophets. As they appeared there in glory, bright and heavenly, yet inferior to the "glory which excelleth," they witnessed that Christ was greater than they. They "appeared in glory," that is, not in fleshly, but glorified spiritual bodies. Moses was commanded to go alone up to the top of Nebo, and die there. Though most diligent search was made, "no man knoweth his sepulchre." Elijah went up in a whirl-

[1] Luke ix. 30, 31.

wind and chariot of fire to heaven. As flesh and blood cannot inherit the kingdom of God, it is scriptural to believe that these worthies were translated, and in the transition received their spiritual bodies. "It is sown in dishonour; it is raised in glory: . . . it is sown a natural body; it is raised a spiritual body. There is a natural body, and there is a spiritual body."[1]

The one absorbing topic of their discourse was "His decease, which He should accomplish at Jerusalem." Their whole thought was intensely fixed upon the death of Christ as an atoning sacrifice. Hence we find that the transfiguration was expressly connected with the time when our Lord took His disciples apart to the regions of Cæsarea Philippi, near the foot of Hermon, to speak to them of His approaching death. And by the symbol of the holy mount Christ shows, that for Him not to die "for sin" would vitiate the prophecies, would be the failure of the plan of redemption, would extinguish every hope of salvation, and would cast over all people the gloom and the impenetrable dark horrors of despair.

[1] I Cor. xv. 43, 44.

Upon this death the confidence of Moses and Elijah, and of all the redeemed then in heaven, rested for their perfect and eternal salvation. In this death all the principalities and powers in the heavenly places were deeply interested. No other topic was so momentous. It filled the hearts of the glorified ones, and until it was accomplished it burdened the heart of our blessed Redeemer. "I have a baptism to be baptized with, and how am I straitened until it be accomplished!"

It may seem strange that Peter and they that were with him were "heavy with sleep." Yet, as the Lord had not given them to expect anything extraordinary in this visit to the mountain, they might have supposed that, as at other times, Jesus came to spend the night in prayer. Being worn out by the duties of the day and the fatigues of the ascent, they yielded to the impulse of wearied nature. Christ did not reprove them for sleeping in the night, the appointed time for sleep. Being asleep they did not see the beginning of the transfiguration—the change from the well-known aspect of His human body to that

Divine effulgence which threw into shadow the brightest shining of the sun. They lost a part, at least, of the conversation between those glorified saints and the Son of God. They heard enough, however, to know what the topic was, and to have their own hearts filled with a heavenly felicity. "And when they were awake, they saw His glory, and the two men that stood with Him."[1] When the heavenly visitors were departing, Peter said, "Master, it is good for us to be here," and proposed the making of "three tabernacles; one for Thee, and one for Moses, and one for Elias: not knowing what he said." The suddenness of the awaking, the intense brilliancy of the scene, amazed him, so that whilst his heart rejoiced his mind was confused, for "they were sore afraid." Had he heard all the conversation, he would more perfectly have understood the necessity of Christ's dying at Jerusalem, and would not have proposed a permanent abode for Him on Mount Hermon.

"While he thus spake, there came a cloud" —a bright cloud, "and overshadowed them:

Luke ix. 32.

and they feared as they entered into the cloud."¹ No wonder that they feared!—this was new and strange experience. The cloud was not that of thick darkness that enshrouded Sinai, but a bright cloud — the symbol of the Divine presence—brighter far than the Shekinah radiance in the Temple. It was not simply beheld, but it enfolded them, enveloped them as in the very embrace of God. "And there came a voice out of the cloud," loud, distinct, penetrating, — "This is My beloved Son: hear Him."² These words being uttered as Moses and Elijah were departing, declared that the promised Messiah, the Prophet like unto Moses and superior to Elijah, had come, and that henceforth to Him, the Son of God, all men must listen, as He is the Prophet, the Priest, and the King of the new dispensation. "When the disciples heard it, they fell on their face, and were sore afraid."³ Human nature could not bear up under such close and overwhelming manifestations of the Divine presence. When Abraham had an interview with God, "an horror of great darkness fell

---

[1] Luke ix. 34.   [2] Luke ix. 35.   [3] Matt. xvii. 6.

upon him."[1] And John says, When I saw "one like unto the Son of man," "I fell at His feet as dead."[2] How long the glorification of Jesus continued it were vain to inquire, nor do we know how long the disciples remained prostrate, chilled, and trembling with fear. We do know that "Jesus came and touched them, and said, Arise, and be not afraid. And when they had lifted up their eyes, they saw no man, save Jesus only."[3] The grandeur and the glory had departed, and Jesus was as aforetime. "And as they came down from the mountain, He charged them that they should tell no man, . . . till the Son of man were risen from the dead." "And they kept it close, and told no man in those days any of those things which they had seen." After the resurrection and ascension, Peter, one of the witnesses, in his Second Epistle, that he might confirm the faith of those to whom he wrote, says : "For we have not followed cunningly devised fables, when we made known unto you the power and coming of our Lord Jesus Christ, but were eye-witnesses of His majesty. For He

[1] Gen. xv. 12.   [2] Rev. i. 17.   [3] Matt. xvii. 7, 8.

received from God the Father honour and glory, when there came such a voice to Him from the excellent glory, This is My beloved Son, in whom I am well pleased. And this voice which came from heaven we heard, when we were with Him in the holy mount." [1]

How strongly does this whole scene impress the conviction that the old and the new dispensation are in perfect harmony with each other, and that the new is the fulfilment and perfection of the old! As no shining glory emanated from Moses and Elijah, and as the voice spake to Jesus only, the new dispensation rises above and supersedes the past. " When the voice was past, Jesus was found alone." How cheering to the hearts of the disciples was this transient glimpse of the glory which awaited their Lord when His work on earth should be done! How calculated to strengthen and comfort their hearts when overborne by persecution to know that the cause would ultimately triumph, and that Jesus would reign supreme, having universal dominion!

[1] 2 Pet. i. 16–18.

VI.

THE MEMORIAL SUPPER.

CHAPTER VI.

THE MEMORIAL SUPPER.

IN all ages memorial structures have been erected. They have stood to perpetuate the memory of some person or event, or as the witness of a covenant. At first they were simple piles of stones, as when Jacob and Laban "took stones and made a heap," and "Laban said, This heap is a witness between me and thee this day. Therefore was the name of it called. . . . Mizpah."[1] So when the children of Israel crossed the Jordan, Joshua commanded them to take twelve stones out of the midst of Jordan, and with them he erected a memorial to perpetuate in Israel the memory of the miraculous crossing of

[1] Gen. xxxi. 48, 49.

the river. As civilisation advanced, these structures became more permanent and ornate. Generally they were erected by a grateful or admiring posterity, as an expression of their estimate of the person or event. Hence have arisen triumphal arches and lofty pillars, equestrian and other statues, monuments and other memorial devices. Where these are prepared by the living to perpetuate their own memory, or placed by survivors in some cathedral, or other receptacle of the dead, the monument will be grand and imposing, according to the wealth and greatness of the person commemorated. The services of the most eminent artists are put in requisition. The most durable materials are employed—marble, granite, gold and silver, bronze, or brass. But they crumble by the tooth of time. They are broken and overthrown by herds of Vandals and the ravages of war. They are destroyed by fire and earthquake. Those that remain are visited by the traveller, but call forth neither love nor friendship. They awaken only admiration, curiosity, or faint remembrances of the person or the event.

In what striking contrast is the memorial supper! "When the hour was come, He sat down, and the twelve apostles with Him. And He said unto them, With desire I have desired to eat this passover with you before I suffer."[1] They knew what He meant by the words "before I suffer." On His last journey from Galilee to Jerusalem He "took the twelve disciples apart in the way, and said unto them, Behold, we go up to Jerusalem ; and the Son of man shall be betrayed unto the chief priests and unto the scribes, and they shall condemn Him to death, and shall deliver Him to the Gentiles to mock, and to scourge, and to crucify Him."[2] Again, "Ye know that after two days is the feast of the passover, and the Son of man is betrayed to be crucified."[3] How impressive His words, "For I say unto you, I will not any more eat thereof, until it be fulfilled in the kingdom of God."[4] "I will not drink henceforth of this fruit of the vine, until that day when I drink it new with you in My Father's kingdom."[5] Knowing, with perfect assur-

---

[1] Luke xxii. 14, 15.   [2] Matt. xx. 17-19.   [3] Matt. xxvi. 2.
[4] Luke xxii. 16.   [5] Matt. xxvi. 29

ance, that His death was near, that it would be the death of a malefactor and a slave, the most ignominious then known, He commanded and provided that the fact that He thus died should be remembered to the end of time. To secure its perpetuation, He erected His own memorial. "He took bread, and gave thanks, and brake it, and gave unto them," His disciples, "saying, This is My body which is given for you: this do in remembrance of Me. Likewise also the cup . . . saying, This cup is the new testament in My blood, which is shed for you."[1] "For as often as ye eat this bread, and drink this cup, ye do show the Lord's death till He come."[2]

Herein, then, lies the difference between Christ's own memorials and the monuments generally reared by men. These are *structures;* that was a *simple act*. The acts, however simple, of which the reason and the motive abide, are calculated to remain in their freshness, unimpaired by age. No age withers them, no custom deadens their interest. It is true that an action which has lost its significance naturally dies out. Some

[1] Luke xxii. 19, 20. [2] 1 Cor. xi. 26.

popular usages to this day retain a fast-vanishing hold upon the community, or have become ludicrous, because unmeaning. But the motives which lead us to break the bread and drink the wine are as freshly felt to-day as when the Master first said, " Do this in remembrance of Me." A monument, again, can occupy but one place. Pilgrims may travel far to visit it; but their view is transient, and to the greater number of men it remains unseen. This memorial of Christ the Saviour is for all parts of the world alike. It belongs to the universal church, and wherever there are the " many members " of the " one body " its significance and tenderness are felt. Where is the nation, where the community, that knows not the use of bread and wine? In all lands the force of the Master's appeal is felt, and in the north and the south, the east and the west, the redeemed family partake together of the supper of the Lord.

Was ever, then, such memorial raised to perpetuate the memory of such an ignominious death? Were ever such frail and perishable materials employed for purposes so lasting ? Whilst the massive monuments built, in His day, of the most enduring materials, have passed away, this endures. After sixty generations it is fresh and quickening as ever, awakening and intensifying love. These simple elements, the bread and the fruit of the vine, form the material for everlasting remembrance. They remain, when stone and metal crumble into dust and perish. This ever-present memorial lifts the worshipper high above the ignominy of the death, to the glorious atoning sacrifice, to the blood shed for the salvation of men. So it can never perish. For as long as men dwell upon the earth they will eat of the bread and drink of the cup which symbolised the death of Jesus as the atoning Saviour and their only hope for salvation. Keeping the feast with loving hearts, each generation will hand it down to the one that follows, until the grand consummation, when all will be gathered to one communion, and drink of the fruit of the vine new and personally with the Mediatorial King in His glory in His Father's kingdom.

VII.

GETHSEMANE.

CHAPTER VII.

GETHSEMANE.

THIS was a garden situated between the brook Kidron and the foot of Mount Olivet, about half a mile from the city wall. The probability is that, in the time of our Lord, it was an olive plantation, as the name Gethsemane signifies an "oil press."

In this garden, to which Christ frequently resorted, occurred one of the most wonderful, soul-stirring, and benevolent scenes in the whole life of the Redeemer. When the supper, the memorial of His coming death, was ended, they sang a hymn, knowing that the hour of His suffering was at hand. Jesus came with His disciples to a place called Gethsemane, and saith to them, "Sit ye here, while I go and pray yonder. And

He took with Him Peter and the two sons of Zebedee," (John and James), the three witnesses of His transfiguration, "and began to be sorrowful, and very heavy," "sore amazed." Leaving the three "He went a little farther," "about a stone's cast, and kneeled down, and prayed, saying, Father, if Thou be willing, remove this cup from Me: nevertheless, not My will, but Thine, be done."[1]

What was this cup, thus referred to? In the Scriptures the term is often used figuratively, signifying great affliction, signal judgments; as "Upon the wicked He shall rain snares, fire and brimstone, and an horrible tempest: this shall be the portion of their cup."[2] "Awake, awake, stand up, O Jerusalem, which hast drunk at the hand of the Lord the cup of His fury; thou hast drunken the dregs of the cup of trembling, and wrung them out."[3] "In the hand of the Lord there is a cup, and the wine is red; it is full of mixture; and He poureth out of the same: but the dregs thereof, all the

---

[1] Matt. xxvi. 36; Mark xiv. 33; Luke xxii. 41.
[2] Psa. xi. 6.   [3] Isa. li. 17.

wicked of the earth shall wring them out, and drink them."[1] The term "cup" is also often used in the Scriptures to denote intense suffering, whether bodily or mental, the greatest which human nature can endure. He looked into the cup which was prepared for Him to drink. He saw, as no one but He could see, the deep unutterable sorrows, the soul-crushing agonies that were in that cup. He saw there the enormous guilt of the whole world. He knew the intensity of its bitterness and woes. He saw sin in its virulence of malignity. He saw the terribleness of its damnation, rolling on through eternal ages with accumulating fierceness and terror. He knew what must be if He drank this cup. He knew that it was the will of His Father that He should drink it. He knew that He had come to drink it. When He contemplated it from the distance, He said, "Now is My soul troubled; and what shall I say? Father, save Me from this hour: but for this cause came I unto this hour. Father, glorify Thy name."[2] Now when the hour had come, and the cup was

[1] Psa. lxxv. 8.   [2] John xii. 27. 28.

no longer contemplated but actual, and to be drunk, and drunk at that time, His human nature, shuddering, quailed. He was oppressed with grief; His soul was overwhelmed with deadly anguish; a grief and anguish intense enough to kill the body. Then His soul was "exceeding sorrowful even unto death;" then He fell upon His face and prayed, "O my Father, if it be possible let this cup pass from Me; nevertheless not as I will, but as Thou wilt." Thus a second time His labouring, sorrowing soul poured out His anguish in holy submission: "O my Father, if this cup may not pass except I drink it, Thy will be done." When there was no lighting up of the intense anguish, no uplifting of the mighty pressure of a world's guilt and ruin, a third time He uttered the same prayer of acquiescing submissive suffering. It was no ordinary grief, no ordinary conflict with the malign "powers of darkness," "the rulers of the darkness of this world," no ordinary upheaving of the soul that drew forth this thrice-repeated piteous prayer; for "His sweat was as it were great drops of blood falling down to the ground." Oh, what an hour of grinding sorrow! He pre-eminently was "a man of sorrows, and acquainted with grief."

What mean these dread upheavals of His sorrowful soul—these mental blood agonies which so crushed His humanity? They were the fulfilment, in part, of the most severely graphic of all the prophetic sufferings of the promised Messiah: "Stricken, smitten of God, and afflicted."[1] The innocent one suffering for the guilty; the just one suffering for the unjust! "Surely He hath borne our griefs, and carried our sorrows." "He was wounded for our trangressions, He was bruised for our iniquities." "Was bruised," literally, *was crushed*. No stronger word can be found in all the Hebrew language to denote the severity of suffering, suffering unto the extinction of life. To this intense prediction of the prophet is the answering record of the evangelist: "My soul is exceeding sorrowful, even unto death."[2] "Being in an agony He prayed more earnestly: and His sweat was as it were great drops of

[1] Isa. liii. 4.   [2] Matt. xxvi. 38.

blood."[1] In the garden "it pleased the Lord to bruise Him; He put Him to grief;" "His soul was made an offering for sin," then He had travail—sore "travail of soul." Here, in these sufferings, not of the body, but mainly of the soul, not for Himself, but for others, is wrought out the grand central essential truth of the Christian system, the expiation of human guilt by the vicarious sufferings of our Lord. "Whom God hath set forth to be a propitiation through faith in His blood, to declare His righteousness for the remission of sins that are past."[2] "He is the propitiation for our sins; and not for ours only, but also for the sins of the whole world."[3]

---

[1] Luke xxii. 44. Some understand "great drops of blood" as figurative, as those who weep bitterly are said to weep tears of blood. Others, with the support of a fact well authenticated, hold that the sweat of our Lord was actually so mixed with blood, that its colour and consistency were as if it had been wholly of blood. The probability of this view is sustained by the statement that Charles IX. of France died of a malady in which his blood gushed out of the pores of his body. Voltaire, in his *Universal History*, thus describes it: "Charles IX. died in his five and twentieth year. The malady he died of was very extraordinary. The blood gushed out of all his pores. This accident, of which there are some instances, was owing either to excessive fear, to violent passion, or to a warm melancholy constitution."

[2] Rom. iii. 25.   [3] 1 John ii. 2.

"Herein is love, not that we loved God, but that He loved us, and sent His Son to be the propitiation for our sins."[1]

In the prophecy of Isaiah, so minutely literal as to be almost historic, words of intensity follow words of increasing strength and weight to express the greatness and severity of the sufferings, as well as their vicarious character. "The chastisement of our peace was upon Him: and with His stripes we are healed." Severely crushing as were the chastisement and the stripes, He could not die there and then. The cross was not yet. It was on the cross He must die, and only on the cross could He say, "The sacrificial work, the travail of My soul, the offering up of My soul for sin, IS FINISHED."

The Scriptures record no sufferings of Christ like those He endured in the garden. On the cross He breathed not a word of sorrow for bodily pain. "About the ninth hour Jesus cried with a loud voice . . . My God, My God, why hast Thou forsaken Me?" This was soul-agony: "Jesus, when He had cried again with a loud voice, yielded up the

[1] 1 John iv. 10.

ghost."[1] This, perhaps, was the keenest and most withering of all His agonies. It filled up to the full the offering of His soul for sin. It was the last great painful anguish of His wearisome travail which, whilst it crushed out His human life, gave life and eternal blessedness to a lost and ruined world. "In Him was life; and the life was the light of men." "I lay down My life for the sheep." "No man taketh it from Me, but I lay it down of Myself." "And I, if I be lifted up from the earth, will draw all men unto Me. This He said, signifying what death He should die."[2]

There is danger of failing to appreciate the full power of His atoning sufferings, by dwelling too stedfastly upon the cross, wonderful as are its tragic scenes and testimonies of love. There is danger, through the over-excited imagination, of being moved mainly by the bodily agonies, and thus throwing into the background the greater and more essential sufferings. It was not His body, but His intelligent soul that was in sore travail, and was made an offering for sin.

[1] Matt. xxvii. 46, 50. [2] John i. 4; x. 15, 18; xii. 32, 33.

What His pure sinless soul suffered for the guilty while on the cross, and what He suffered in the wilderness and in the garden, should command the most earnest thought, the deepest veneration, and the most adoring devotion. What He endured of exhaustion and suffering when buffeted by Satan forty days and forty nights, we have no record. That it was intensely severe we know from the persistent malignity of the tempter, and from the fact that when it ended, angels ministered unto Him. In the garden, when mental anguish permeated His soul, He endured more of vicarious suffering than at any other time, save only when, on the cross, that bitter cry of agony was wrenched out, " My God, My God, why hast Thou forsaken Me ?" In the wilderness He was alone; in the garden He was alone; on the cross He was alone. " He trod the winepress alone; and of the people there was none with Him."

To use a very homely illustration,—as the value of a bank-note is not in the size of the paper, or the amount of printing thereon, but only in the character which is stamped upon it, of ten, one hundred, or one thousand, so the value of vicarious sufferings is not determined by their length or severity, but by the character of the sufferer. "Ye were not redeemed with corruptible things, as silver and gold . . . but with the precious blood of Christ, as of a lamb without blemish and without spot: who verily was foreordained before the foundation of the world, but was manifest in these last times for you."[1] "Thou wast slain, and hast redeemed us to God by thy blood out of every kindred, and tongue, and people, and nation,"[2] is the grateful homage and the triumphant ceaseless song of the redeemed.

The question, What means this thrice-repeated prayer? comes again to the front with the anxious inquiry, Was it heard, *and answered?* Did not the Lord Jesus know whether His petition were possible? Could He pray for that which was impossible? Were the requisite qualifications for the certain answer to prayer not found in Him? Neither of these suppositions can for a moment be entertained. Then whence this failing of heart, this sore amazement, this pressure of sorrow, which brought

[1] 1 Pet. i. 18–20.   [2] Rev. v. 9.

Him nigh unto death, which so prostrated His body and soul and spirit as to force from Him the bloody sweat? Was it the mere dread of death? Death came by sin; but He knew no sin. Being pure and innocent, death had no claims upon Him, and He could not dread a future reckoning. Was it the dread of the bodily tortures of His approaching crucifixion — so full of human and satanic malignity, and treachery, and weariness, and scourging, and ignominy, and suffering? Certainly not, for multitudes of His followers have met all these with "unshaken cheerfulness." Make His sufferings as terrible as possible, and with every aggravating circumstance, and still, for Jesus to shrink and pray for deliverance at the prospect of them, would show a weakness to which very many of His disciples, supported by His grace and presence, were strangers. They cheerfully, and without the least emotion, endured, for His sake, the most terrible of deaths. It was not this apprehension, which in all its "horror of great darkness" He perfectly foreknew and comprehended. It was something infinitely more than this; something far more deadly than this. It was, as we have already stated, the burden of the world's sin, which lay so heavy upon His generous, sensitive heart. It was the drinking of the bitter cup which sin had poisoned.

The apostle, when reviewing this hour in the garden, says: "Who in the days of His flesh, when He had offered up prayers and supplications with strong crying and tears unto Him that was able to save Him from death, and was heard in that He feared."[1] This passage illuminates that dark, intensely dark, hour of Christ's mighty sorrow. It tells us what Jesus then feared. It was death. It tells us what He prayed for. It was deliverance from death. It tells us that the prayer was heard, and that it was heard because Jesus feared death. That it was heard means that it was answered. At the tomb of Lazarus, Jesus "groaned in spirit, and was troubled;" then "Jesus lifted up His eyes, and said, Father, I thank Thee that

---

[1] Heb. v. 7; which may perhaps be read, "heard (and delivered) from His fear." The ellipsis is like that in Psa. xxii. 21, "Thou hast heard (and delivered) me from the horns of the unicorns."

Thou hast heard Me. And I knew that Thou hearest Me always."

There the answer was immediate. So here, Christ was heard and answered when He prayed in the garden. What He then feared was death, not on His own account, not because of the dread anticipated sufferings, for these He did endure, "being obedient unto death, even the death of the cross." What He feared was, that His human nature would *then* sink crushed under the terrific pressure, in this hour of His great suffering. Should He be thus crushed, His great work of atonement, which must be on the cross, would fail. Therefore He feared death, and prayed to Him who "was able to save Him from death"—prayed that He *might not die then and there*, but that He might live, and go on to suffer and to complete, on the cross, the work which His Father gave Him to do. How apposite and definite this prayer: "And prayed that, if it were possible, the *hour* might pass from Him."[1] The present hour, not that of the cross. The hour of suffering, aggravated, may be, by the

[1] Mark xiv. 35.

malignant assault of the devil, who, though he failed in the wilderness, "departed from Him for a season"[1] only, tempting Him to abandon such sufferings on behalf of such worthless, guilty wretches as men.

His prayer had an immediate answer; for when He lay prostrate upon the earth, in the deep throes of His deadly anguish, and sweating as it were great drops of blood, there "appeared an angel unto Him, strengthening Him."[2] The hour passed, His agony ceased, and He met His betrayer. But for this timely supernatural strengthening, His human nature would have sunk under the pressure of mental and soul agonies. When for forty days He fasted, and was tempted of the devil, "angels came and ministered unto Him." Thus in the garden, by supernatural power, He was strengthened and saved from death at that time. He lived and, with no evidence of weakness, went through all the subsequent trials and sufferings, until upon the cross He could say, "It is finished;" then "He bowed His head, and gave up the ghost."

[1] Luke iv. 13.   [2] Luke xxii. 43.

What He asked He knew was agreeable to the will of His Father. He came to suffer in the garden and on the cross. This was the will of God. He prayed that the will of God might be done. He prayed that His body might not die in the garden when on the way to the cross; but that He might live until the whole work of atoning suffering was done. This prayer was not selfish, but glowing with benevolence, and He knew that it was agreeable to the Divine will; and it was heard and answered. It is recorded, not as some teach, simply as an example of submission to unanswered prayer, but as an encouragement to pray with the assurance that, having the qualifications for true prayer, the prayer will be answered. That it teaches cheerful submission, even in the darkest hour, is certain. It does more: it calls us to remember with adoring gratitude the benevolence of Christ, praying that He might be sustained to endure and live to suffer until His finished sufferings secured the salvation of men. In all our trials we are assured of His sympathy. The remembrance of His own " prayers and supplications, with strong crying and tears," and the supernatural help then given Him, will ever keep His heart alive to the earnest cries of His people, when they, quickened by the Holy Spirit, plead for things agreeable to the Divine will.

VIII.

THE BETRAYAL.

CHAPTER VIII.

THE BETRAYAL.

THE agonies of the garden being ended, the soul of the Redeemer was filled with a heavenly calm. Being strengthened by the ministering angel, He arose, firm and resolute. He set Himself, with irresistible determination, to go on to the death which He knew was nigh. He came to His disciples, saying, "The hour is at hand, and the Son of man is betrayed into the hands of sinners. Rise, let us be going: behold, he is at hand that doth betray Me."[1] No fear disturbed Him; His courage was unshaken; He went forth, a willing sacrifice. "And while He yet spake, lo, Judas, one of the twelve, came, and with him a great mul-

[1] Matt. xxvi. 45, 46.

titude with swords and staves, from the chief priests and elders of the people."[1] "Judas knew the place: for Jesus ofttimes resorted thither with His disciples."[2] The chief priests and elders being informed that the time had come to carry out their concerted plan, they obtained a band, the captain and officers of the temple guard, who came with lanterns and torches and weapons.

The priests and elders prepared this array, either to secure themselves against any commotion, or to make it appear that Jesus was a dangerous ringleader of sedition. "Jesus therefore, knowing all things that should come upon Him, went forth" to meet these armed men, and "said unto them, Whom seek ye? They answered Him, Jesus of Nazareth." With heroic frankness, "Jesus saith unto them, I am He."[3] There was something in the manner of Jesus which arrested their advance—"they went backward;" something that so filled them with awe and dread that they "fell to the ground." What was this something? Did the calm majesty and benignity of His countenance

[1] Matt. xxvi. 47.   [2] John xviii. 2.   [3] John xviii. 4, 5.

strike home the conviction that He was a holy and innocent man? Or did His Divinity flash out for a moment with withering power? There they would have remained, like dead men, had not Jesus summoned them to consciousness by asking again, "Whom seek ye? And they said, Jesus of Nazareth. Jesus answered, I have told you that I am He." He thus expressed a second time His willingness to be apprehended by them. But though ready to be offered Himself, His kind heart pleaded for His disciples: "If therefore ye seek Me, let these go their way." This request He made to the soldiers whose business it was to arrest Him.

The narrative particularly states that "Judas also, which betrayed Him, stood with them,"—not awestruck and overpowered, as were the soldiers, but rigidly determined to carry out his part of the compact. As the soldiers did not personally know Jesus, and as, in the darkness and confusion, they might not seize the right person, a certain sign had been agreed on. "Whomsoever I shall kiss, that same is He: hold Him fast;"[1] "take

[1] Matt. xxvi. 48.

Him, and lead Him away." "And he came to Jesus, and said, Hail, Master; and kissed Him."

"And Jesus said unto him, Friend, wherefore art thou come?" Friend! this implied neither approbation nor complacency in the act. Rather was it the severest possible rebuke. "Judas, thou comest to Me joyfully, saying, All hail! Thou callest Me Master, declaring My superiority and your confidence in Me; thou givest Me a kiss, the token of the most intimate and sacred friendship; and lo! this is the concerted token of your treachery. I am not taken by surprise. I knew you would seek for Me in this retired garden, whither I often came with My disciples. I have come to meet you here. I have not been deceived. I knew that you had a devil; that you were covetous and resentful; yet I took you into My family, and placed you under the very best circumstances for becoming a good man. You saw My miracles, you heard My teachings, you knew My whole manner of life; you were the equal companion of true and loyal men; and through the years I treated you with the same external confidence that

I did the others. I gave you warning when we were all gathered at the last passover, saying 'that one of you should betray Me;' 'the hand of him that betrayeth Me is with me on the table.' When, in deep sorrow, each said, 'Lord, is it I?' rather suspecting themselves than you, I told them, 'He that dippeth with Me in the dish, the same shall betray Me.' Then when you, at the last, said, 'Master, is it I?' I frankly answered, 'Thou hast said.' Still more faithfully and pointedly did I warn you when the beloved John asked, 'Who is it?' I said, 'He it is to whom I shall give a sop when I have dipped it.' With bated breath and searching eyes, and anxiety on every countenance, they watched Me; then I dipped the sop and gave it to you, and I told you of the terrible doom which awaited you if you should persevere in your wicked purpose: 'The Son of man goeth, as it is written of Him: but woe to that man by whom the Son of man is betrayed! good were it for that man if he had never been born.' You then left Me and your fellow-disciples; you hurried to the chief priests and elders, and covenanted with them for thirty pieces of silver to deliver Me into their hands. And now you have come with armed men, as though I were a man of desperate wickedness. You have sold Me at the price of a slave. I am neither surprised nor deceived."

Why did He not spurn the wretch with holy indignation? Meekness and gentleness prevailed. What wonderful self-control! He knew what the end would be. He left it to time and the pungency of conscience and remorse to proclaim His innocence and to bring about the earthly end of the betrayer. "Then Judas, which had betrayed Him . . . brought again the thirty pieces of silver to the chief priests and elders, saying, I have sinned in that I have betrayed the innocent blood." When they replied, "What is that to us? see thou to that," "he cast down the pieces of silver in the Temple, and departed, and went and hanged himself." Truly, "the way of transgressors is hard." Than the suicide of an apostle what could be more awful? Or what could teach a more salutary lesson to ourselves, to take heed lest we fall, and ourselves betray our Lord?

"Then the band and the captain and officers of the Jews took Jesus and bound Him." Peter had looked on with strange emotion, wondering whereunto these things would grow. But when they seized and bound Jesus, his swelling emotions culminated. He could restrain himself no longer. He "drew his sword, and struck a servant of the high priest's, and smote off his ear."[1] This was the beginning of strife, and how bloody and deadly would have been the result cannot be told, had not Jesus, with authority, commanded, "Put up thy sword;" "the cup which My Father hath given Me, shall I not drink it?" This arrested the turbulent Peter. Benevolently touching the ear, Christ healed it; and this quieted the soldiers. It is strange that this miracle of healing made no salutary impression upon the priests and elders and captains of the Temple. He now referred them to His daily works and teachings in the Temple, when they stretched forth no hand against Him. But now "Are ye come out as against a thief with swords and staves for to take Me?" "This is your hour, and

[1] Matt. xxvi. 51.

the power of darkness."[1] He yielded peacefully, not because He was feeble and unprotected: "Thinkest thou that I cannot now pray to My Father, and He shall presently give Me more than twelve legions of angels? But how then shall the scriptures be fulfilled, that thus it must be?"[2] "All things must be fulfilled, which were written in the law of Moses, and in the prophets, and in the psalms, concerning Me."[3]

"They bound Him." It was not the cord that held Him; this He could have broken with infinite ease. It was not the band of soldiers that restrained Him; these He could have struck dead as promptly as He threw them upon the ground. His immense, unconquerable love was stronger than the cord, was mightier than the armed band. Strange, passing strange, that, when the disciples saw that the men of violence had the mastery, they "all forsook Him, and fled!"[4]

[1] Luke xxii. 53.
[2] Matt. xxvi. 53, 54.
[3] Luke xxiv. 44.
[4] Matt. xxvi. 56.

IX.

THE TRIAL.

CHAPTER IX.

THE TRIAL.

BEFORE THE PRIESTS.

Bound and closely guarded, the exultant crowd "led Him away to Annas first," the father-in-law of Caiaphas. Though deposed from the high priesthood by the Roman procurator Valerius, he still retained the title. From the mention made of him in Luke iii. 2, John xviii. 13, and Acts iv. 6, it is probable that he continued to act as a sagan, or deputy.

Why Jesus was first brought to Annas is not stated. As it was now fully midnight, and as no legal council could meet at that hour, He may have been lodged there primarily for safe-keeping. Annas availed himself of this opportunity, and "asked Jesus of His disciples, and of His doctrine;" that is, "Who are Thy disciples, and for what end hast Thou gathered them? Is it to make Thyself a king? And what are the doctrines Thou hast taught them?" These questions were artfully framed, so as to lead Christ to declare Himself to be the Messiah. Judging by himself, and supposing Christ to be actuated by worldly ambition, he expected He would admit this claim, and thus would be condemned on His own confession.

Whilst the answer of Jesus was calm and dignified, it administered a decided reproof: "I spake openly to the world; I ever taught in the synagogue, and in the Temple, whither the Jews always resort; and in secret have I said nothing. Why askest thou Me? Ask them which heard Me, what I have said unto them: behold, they know what I said." This was so obviously just that it uncovered the iniquity of this attempt to make Christ convict Himself. But it only stirred up wrath. "When He had thus spoken, one of the officers which stood by struck Jesus with the palm of his hand, saying, Answerest thou the high priest so?"

Annas did not reprove this illegal insolence, but by his silence encouraged it. Paul, when smitten on the mouth by the command of Ananias—thus illegally deciding the case before it was heard—roused up into sudden anger, said, "God shall smite thee, thou whited wall: for sittest thou to judge me after the law, and commandest me to be smitten contrary to the law?" When those who stood by said, "Revilest thou God's high priest?" he justified himself, saying, "I wist not, brethren, that he was the high priest." It was notorious that Ananias was not called to that office in accordance with the Divine law, but that all the authority which he had was derived from the Roman political power. And yet the apostle recognised the reverence due to the office; for it is written, "Thou shalt not speak evil of the ruler of thy people." But Jesus, the infinitely more insulted one, with no indication of anger or of holy indignation, meekly reproved the offender, saying, "If I have spoken evil, bear witness of the evil: but if well, why smitest thou Me?"

This examination before Annas is only

related by the evangelist John. It demonstrates the temper and determination of those by whose authority He was arrested. They seized Him with a foregone determination that He should be put to death. The narrative leaves the impression on the mind that Annas, though deposed, yet by reason of his age and worldly position, had controlling influence, and was really the most guilty of all concerned in securing the death of Jesus. Being satisfied that he could not extort from the prisoner any self-conviction, he sent Him bound to Caiaphas the high priest.

"As soon as it was day, the elders of the people and the chief priests and the scribes came together, and led him into their council." In scanning the parties who composed this council, it is worthy of note that no mention is made of the Pharisees. This is the more remarkable, when we call to mind their undisguised hatred of Christ, and their persevering endeavours to entrap Him by various subtleties. As we cannot suppose they were averse to His being put to death, their absence may be accounted for by their opposition to the Sadducees, who were the dominant party, having the high priesthood and the control of the Sanhedrim.

As Jesus, in His examination before Annas, told him that the proper method of procedure was to summon witnesses to prove what doctrine He had taught, so "the council sought false witnesses against Jesus, to put Him to death." They had determined upon His death; but the forms of law must be observed. As no true witnesses could be brought to testify against Him, they had resort to false ones. This, at that day, as well as at the present, was practised by unscrupulous men. In the case of Stephen, when the council were not able to resist the wisdom and the spirit by which he spake, they suborned men. The witnesses summoned by Caiaphas, "though many," were useless: "but their witness agreed not together." Their language and bearing were contemptuous. "This fellow said, I am able to destroy the temple of God, and to build it in three days." When the high priest saw that Jesus took no notice of the things witnessed, "he arose, and said unto Him, Answerest Thou nothing? What is it which these witness against Thee? But Jesus held His peace, and answered nothing." "Who, when He was reviled, reviled not again; when He suffered, He threatened not; but committed Himself to Him that judgeth righteously."

Thwarted and chagrined by the failure of the witnesses, and by the silence and dignified composure of Jesus, the high priest, endeavouring to force out of Him some confession on which he might condemn Him, said, "Art Thou the Christ? tell us." Jesus replied, "If I tell you, ye will not believe: and if I also ask you, ye will not answer Me, nor let Me go." This was plain and honest. It clearly intimated that He perfectly understood the temper and determination of the court before which He stood, and that it would avail nothing for Him to plead. Reduced to utter despair, this false high priest made one more desperate effort to wrench out a confession by which to condemn Him. Still standing, and with all the high influence of his office concentrated in his manner and words, said, "I adjure Thee, by the living God, that Thou tell us whether Thou be the Christ, the

Son of God," "the Son of the Blessed." Strange question this from the judge, who, with impartial justice, should protect the rights of the prisoner! Strange question to be put to a prisoner bound and defenceless, and virtually condemned, though nothing had been proved against Him! But not strange, under the circumstances, when all the forms of law had failed. Being thus adjured, the Jewish equivalent to being under oath, Jesus could no longer be silent or allow of any misunderstanding of His true position. Knowing that death was near, and would be made certain by His truthful answer, He hesitated not a moment, but firmly replied, "Thou hast said." "I am." And, with deep solemnity, He added, "Hereafter shall ye see the Son of man sitting on the right hand of power, and coming in the clouds of heaven." "Then the high priest rent his clothes"—the token of his sacred horror, "saying, He hath spoken blasphemy; what further need have we of witnesses?" Having thus convicted Him by His words of truth, the high priest said, "Now ye have heard His blasphemy. What think ye? They answered and said,

He is guilty of death." "And they all condemned Him to be guilty of death." A just appreciation of this solemn hour, when a man is condemned to death, should hush any angry feeling and subdue every turbulent emotion. Not so now; this was the hour of triumph for the powers of darkness, when the malice and the scorn which had long been pent up found free utterance. "Then did they spit in His face;" "they mocked" and "buffeted Him." Bound and helpless, they blindfolded Him, and, with derision, " smote Him with the palms of their hands, saying, Prophesy unto us, Thou Christ, Who is he that smote Thee? And many other things blasphemously spake they against Him."

BEFORE PILATE.

The scene now changes from the Jewish to the Gentile tribunal. "When the morning was come, all the chief priests and elders of the people took counsel against Jesus to put Him to death: and when they had bound Him, they led Him away, and delivered Him to Pontius Pilate the governor."

Pontius Pilate was the sixth Roman Procurator of Judea, having his usual residence in Cæsarea. By reason of his cruelties and oppressions he had become, not only unpopular, but decidedly odious to the Jews, and especially to the Samaritans, whose blood "he mingled with their sacrifices."

It is worthy of note that the apostles expressed no intense condemnation of Pilate when they charged the murder of Christ upon the Jewish rulers. They simply state the fact that "before Pontius Pilate He witnessed a good confession," and that "Pilate delivered Him to be crucified." Our Lord discriminated the relative guilt of the several parties, saying, "He that delivered Me unto thee hath the greater sin." That the conduct of Pilate was highly criminal cannot be denied. Yet it was light compared with that of the priests. His was the guilt of weakness and fear; theirs of settled and deliberate malice and murder. In his hands was the life of the prisoner. He believed Him to be innocent. He should have set Him at liberty, regardless of consequences; but he yielded to violence and regard to personal interest, and so committed an awful crime. A careful and candid collation of all the facts show that, vicious and cruel and unjust as Pilate was in his usual conduct, in the trial of Christ he made repeated and strenuous efforts to protect and defend Him, an innocent man, against the malice of His enemies.

Immediately after the examination of Jesus before the council, where, on an extorted confession, they pronounced Him guilty of blasphemy, they led Him, the priests accompanying, from Caiaphas to the hall of judgment, or Prætorium. This was the residence of the Roman governor when in Jerusalem, which was always at the passover and other festal gatherings. It was probably in the Castle of Antonia, in the north-west corner of the Temple area. Here the Roman soldiers were in garrison.[1] Here occurs the strangest regard for the minutest items of the ceremonial law, whilst the priests were perseveringly trampling on all justice and all mercy. Having purified themselves, they would not enter into the palace, the house of a heathen. "They themselves went not into the judgment hall, lest they should be de-

[1] Mark xv. 16; Acts xxi. 31-37; xxiii. 10.

filed." "Ye pay tithe of mint and anise and cummin, and have omitted the weightier matters of the law, judgment, mercy, and faith." "Pilate then went out unto them, and said, What accusation bring ye against this man?" This question, perfectly proper for the judge to ask, took them by surprise. Pilate intended a judicial inquiry, but they expected him simply to give the order for His execution. Being offended, and throwing themselves upon their dignity, they replied, "If He were not a malefactor, we would not have delivered Him unto thee." It may be that Pilate spake in a manner so stern and authoritative as to show his displeasure for bringing to him a person to be sentenced to death against whom no sufficient accusation and proof had been brought. He would not be an executioner where he had not been a judge. Perhaps with manifested contempt, he said, "Take ye Him, and judge Him according to your law." Now they are compelled to confess their national humiliation, that they could not inflict the death-penalty. "It is not lawful for us to put any man to death." The Jewish law made stoning the punishment for blasphemy: "He that blasphemeth the name of the Lord, he shall surely be put to death, and all the congregation shall certainly stone him."[1] For other crimes, hanging was the penalty. "If a man have committed a sin worthy of death ... and thou hang him on a tree."[2] But the power of life and death had been taken from the Jews by their Roman masters. Such cases as the stoning of Stephen were wild, tumultuary proceedings, out of the course of law. By being thus compelled to refer the matter to the heathen authorities, the Jews unconsciously fulfilled the prophetic words of Jesus: "Shall deliver Him to the Gentiles, to mock, and to scourge, and to crucify Him." "And I, if I be lifted up from the earth, will draw all men unto Me. This He spake, signifying what death He should die."

Having failed in their first effort, they abandon the charge of blasphemy, and resort to definite accusations. These are so framed as to compel Pilate to entertain them. "And they began to accuse Him, saying, We found this fellow perverting the nation, and for-

[1] Lev. xxiv. 16.   [2] Deut. xxi. 22.

bidding to give tribute to Cæsar, saying that He Himself is Christ a King." Here are three political crimes: perverting the nation, withholding tribute, and proclaiming Himself to be the Messiah—a king, the King of the Jews. How artful are these charges; how well calculated to excite the jealousy of the judge! Pilate, that he might not seem to fail in loyalty to the Roman emperor, "entered into the judgment hall again, and called Jesus unto him, and," passing by the first and second charges as of less moment, "said unto Him, Art Thou the King of the Jews?" There is no evidence of agitation, or of severity, or suspicion on the part of Pilate, but rather of confidence in Jesus that He would tell the truth. As by the Roman law no prisoner was compelled to accuse himself, Christ might have refused to answer. Had He said No, it would have been untrue. Had He said Yes, without any explanation, it would have misled the governor. "Jesus said unto him, Thou sayest it,"—it is as thou sayest. Then He asks a question, justified by Roman law, which secured to Him the right to know and to face His accusers:

"Sayest thou this thing of thyself, or did others tell it thee of Me?" Pilate, perhaps with scornful contempt, answered, "Am I a Jew?" Is it probable that I, a Gentile, am personally acquainted with the religious opinions, expectations, and disputes of your people? The accusation does not come from me. " Thine own nation and the chief priests have delivered Thee unto me;" they are your accusers. "What hast thou done?" He might with justice have replied, What says My life? My teachings have ever been in the synagogues and the Temple, open to all persons. Let those who have heard Me testify. *What have I done?* Many works of healing and of mercy. They have not been done in secret places, but openly, in Judea, in Samaria, and in Galilee; let the healed ones and their friends and the bystanders bear witness of what I have done. Do these indicate that I am a turbulent person, or that I have stirred up the people to treasonable acts? I have said I am a King. "My kingdom is not of this world." I interfere not with your authority; I am not an enemy to Cæsar; I assume no worldly station. "If My kingdom were of this world, then would My servants fight, that I should not be delivered to the Jews." So far from this, I restrained one of My disciples from fighting when he drew his sword and smote off the ear of the servant of the high priest. He would have rescued Me from the armed band, but I forbade him; and, to redress the evil he had done, I healed the wounded man, and then quietly submitted to be bound and led away. Pilate could neither understand nor reconcile statements like these with His claim to be a king. He repeats the question, "Art Thou a king then?" "Jesus answered, Thou sayest that I am a king;" it is as thou sayest,—I am a king; "to this end was I born, and for this cause came I into the world, that I should bear witness unto the truth. Every one that is of the truth heareth My voice." This is what Paul calls the "good confession" which Christ Jesus witnessed before Pontius Pilate. The words are of the profoundest meaning. Our Lord declares, not only that He uttered the truth in claiming royalty, but that His kingdom has its only foundation in THE TRUTH. His witness to this made Him King—enthroned in the believing hearts and consenting wills of men. Thus He reigns. He is Himself the Truth. "The truth is in Jesus."

It is observable that Pilate was not offended by this claim to royalty on the part of Christ. It may be that when our Lord spake of bearing witness to the truth, adding, that every one that is of the truth would hear His voice and follow Him, Pilate supposed Him to be some philosopher, whose claim to royalty must be mystically understood. Hence "Pilate saith unto Him, What is truth?" To this question, which may have been asked because he was indifferent to any further prosecution of the trial, Jesus made no reply. And when "the chief priests accused Him of many things, He answered nothing." "Then said Pilate unto Him, Hearest Thou not how many things they witness against Thee? And He answered him to never a word; insomuch that the governor marvelled greatly." "He was oppressed, and He was afflicted, yet He opened not His mouth: He is brought as a lamb to the slaughter, and as a sheep before

---

[1] See John xiv. 6; Eph. iv. 21.

her shearers is dumb, so He opened not His mouth."

Then "Pilate went out again unto the Jews, and said to the chief priests and to the people, *I find no fault in this man*." Having made this decision, he should at once have caused Jesus to be unbound and released from the custody of the priests with their armed band. Why he did not may not certainly be known. His previous conduct towards the Jews, and a recollection of the influence which their rulers had at Rome, may have made him reluctant to excite their wrath.

BEFORE HEROD.

When Pilate pronounced Christ to be innocent of the three charges, the priests were not satisfied. It was not what they expected and were determined to have. It only kindled their wrath into a fiercer flame, and their voices rose in wilder tumult. "And they were the more fierce:" they reiterated the charges with more intense emphasis: "He stirreth up the people, teaching throughout all Jewry, beginning from Galilee to this place." Very artfully do they mention Galilee as the starting-place of the sedition; for they knew that Galilee was under the jurisdiction of Herod, and also that Pilate and Herod were at enmity with each other. Amid the clamorous and passionate accusations the word Galilee caught the ear of Pilate, and "he asked whether the man were a Galilean. And as soon as he knew that He belonged to Herod's jurisdiction, he sent Him to Herod, who himself also was at Jerusalem at that time." Pilate's motive may have been that Herod, being the prince of that region, would have the means of certain knowledge concerning the charge of sedition. As Herod was a Jew, he would be conversant with the laws and customs of his nation. At any rate, if Herod should condemn Christ, Pilate would escape the guilt and infamy of putting to death an innocent man. Whatever the motive was, Christ, still bound, was sent to Herod. This was Herod Antipas, the son of Herod the Great, and governor of Galilee and Peræa. He lived in adultery with Herodias, the wife of his brother Philip; and, instigated by this base woman, because rebuked by John the Baptist, had caused him to be beheaded. He was naturally of a weak, mild temperament, but cunning, dissolute, and selfishly cruel. It was of this man, when "certain of the Pharisees came unto Christ, saying unto Him, Get thee out, and depart hence [Peræa]: for Herod will kill Thee," that He replied, "Go ye, and tell that fox, Behold, I cast out devils, and I do cures to-day and to-morrow, and the third day I shall be perfected." This Herod was of the sect of the Sadducees, who denied the immortality of the soul and disbelieved in future punishment. He was thus in sympathy with the high priests and majority of the Sanhedrim, who also were Sadducees. This is the man to whom Pilate sent Jesus.

"And when Herod saw Jesus, he was exceeding glad." He was glad, not that he might be taught and led in the right way; not that he might have the opportunity to defend the rights of an injured innocent man; but that curiosity, his love of the marvellous, might be gratified, "for he was desirous to see Him of a long season,[1] because he had

[1] Luke ix. 9.

heard many things of Him; and he hoped to have seen some miracle done by Him." Prompt and liberal as Christ was in His miracles for the poor and afflicted, He would not work one to gratify the curiosity of this man, before whom He stood as a prisoner charged with sedition and treason. Disappointed of the miracle, " he questioned with Him in many words." These probably were vexatious questions, designed to entrap Him. Meanwhile "the chief priests and scribes stood and vehemently accused Him." But our Lord maintained the majesty of silence: " He answered him nothing." Then the vulgar insolence of Herod's nature broke forth. " And Herod with his men of war set Him at nought, and mocked Him." They derided and treated Him with the utmost contempt and insolence. They " arrayed Him in a gorgeous robe," a white robe, the royal colour among the Hebrews. Thus they mocked His claims to royalty and to innocence. Disappointed as Herod was, and sympathising with the Jews in their hatred to Christ, still he did not dare to condemn Him on the charges preferred, for he knew that no sedition had been stirred by Him in Galilee. He "sent Him again to Pilate. And the same day Pilate and Herod were made friends together: for before they were at enmity between themselves." It was not a common hatred of Jesus that made them friends, as is often supposed, for Pilate manifested no personal hatred, but a strong and persistent desire to deliver Him. It was rather the act of courtesy on the part of Pilate in recognising the jurisdiction of Herod, and in sending Christ for his judgment, that healed their animosity.

AGAIN BEFORE PILATE.

"And Pilate, when he had called together the chief priests and the rulers and the people, said unto them, Ye have brought this man unto me, as one that perverteth the people: and, behold, I, having examined Him before you, have found no fault in this man touching those things whereof ye accuse Him: no, nor yet Herod: for I sent you to him; and, lo, nothing worthy of death is done unto Him. I will therefore chastise Him, and release Him." How strange this conclusion, after so clear a conviction of the perfect innocence of Jesus! Having, as His judge, pronounced Him absolutely innocent, he should have set Him absolutely free. Why chastise Him? He saw the determined purpose of the priests and rulers; he saw the gathering crowds of excited people, and he feared this accumulated power. To justify them in bringing Christ before him, and to please them by rendering ridiculous the pretensions of Jesus to royalty, and to ruin Him by a disgraceful public infliction, he proposes to chastise Him, and then set Him free. This did not suit the high priests and rulers. It was not His disgrace, but His death as a malefactor, that they wanted, and would have.

JESUS OR BARABBAS?

It was the custom of the governor, on the occasion of the Passover, to release the prisoner whom the people might desire. Pilate therefore asked, "Will ye that I release unto you the King of the Jews?" This question he addressed to the people, with the hope that they, remembering the many miracles

Christ had wrought, and knowing that no accusation against Him had been proved, would select Him as the prisoner to be released. He took this course the more confidently because he knew "that the chief priests had delivered Him for envy."

There was a prisoner named Barabbas, "who had made insurrection,"—the crime they charged against Jesus,—"who had committed murder." He was the leader of a dangerous band, in character and behaviour the very opposite of Christ. "Whom will ye that I release unto you, Barabbas, or Jesus which is called Christ?" It is not improbable that Barabbas, himself already condemned, was present, and stood contrasted with Jesus.

At this critical moment a messenger hurries into the court and hastily approaches the governor. All proceedings are stayed. The governor, with great excitement, receives the message. It is from his wife, Claudia Procula, who, being greatly troubled, and having "suffered many things this day in a dream because of Him" (Jesus), importuned the governor to "have nothing to do with that just man."[1] The people of that era believed in dreams, especially those of the morning hour, as omens or warnings. For the time this message staggered him. He paused, and deliberated what he should do—how he should release the prisoner, and not exasperate the high priests, and still more inflame the populace. During this pause the priests and rulers were not idle. They were busy among the people, who had not yet replied and expressed their choice. "But the chief priests and elders persuaded the multitude that they should ask Barabbas, and destroy Jesus." Having resumed the trial, the governor asked, "Whether of the twain will ye that I release unto you?" "And they cried out all at once, Away with this man, and release unto us Barabbas." The governor was disappointed. He supposed that the people would, through their dread of a robber and murderer, desire the release of Christ. But then, even as now, the masses blindly follow the leaders who inflame their prejudices

---

[1] The fact that the wife of Pilate was then in Jerusalem illustrates the accuracy of the Gospel records, as the provincial governors had but recently been allowed by the Roman Senate to have their wives with them.

and blind their judgment. "Pilate therefore, willing to release Jesus, spake again to them, What will ye that I shall do unto Him whom ye call the King of the Jews?" What a moment of supreme, intense interest! What glances of malignant fire shot from the eyes of the high priests and elders, to exasperate the people and hold them to their dread work! Would they stand firm, or would they shrink from the fearful leap into the guilt of demanding the death of the man whom the judge had repeatedly declared to be innocent, in whom he "found no fault at all?"

Stealthily there move among the multitude the desperate and determined leaders, whispering here and urging there, until a voice, clear, shrill, and piercing, strikes the keynote, "Crucify Him!" At this response Pilate expressed his surprise, and puts in a plea for the prisoner, "Why, what evil hath He done? I have found no cause of death in Him: I will therefore chastise Him, and let Him go." Now was the critical moment. Pilate pleads for Him, and the people hesitate. It is now or never. The leaders, who must either triumph or perish, make their last appeal. They stir up the depths and succeed: " They cried out the more," "more exceedingly," "instant with loud voices, Crucify Him!" "And the voices of them and of the chief priests prevailed." How intense that malignity which rejects all evidence, which tramples out all pleadings of humanity, and which, with undeviating tenacity, demands the death of an innocent man! How bitterly cruel is envy! How terrific the control of evil-minded leaders over the ignorant and the prejudiced!

"When Pilate saw that he could prevail nothing, but rather that a tumult was made," for it was not the deliberate voice of the people, but a blind uproar, inflamed and guided by wicked selfish leaders, "he took water, and washed his hands before the multitude, saying, I am innocent of the blood of this just person: see ye to it." He may have performed this in accordance with the heathen rite, which prescribed lustrations for such as innocently or unwillingly had committed murder. Or it might be that he intended to impress the people that he acted in keeping with their own laws, which required, in the case of an unknown murder, the elders of the nearest city to wash their hands publicly, and say, "Our hands have not shed this blood."

By this impressive act Pilate intended to express his solemn conviction of the innocence of Christ, that he had done all he could to save Him, and that he only yielded to the forces that surrounded and coerced him. Thus he would throw off from himself, and upon the accusers, all the guilt of putting this innocent man to death. Fatal delusion! There is no possible transference of guilt from one man to another man. When Pilate added, "See ye to it," and thus devolved the responsibility on them, he hoped to arrest them in their bold determination. It was unavailing. The inflexible leaders had caused the people so publicly to commit themselves that they were ready to assume any and all the responsibility. Then, with unparalleled infatuation, "answered all the people, and said, His blood be on us, and on our children." Terrific imprecation! God does answer the prayers of wicked men. The answer to this prayer has, for eighteen centuries, been the doom of the Jewish race. To this day they are under the curse of their own imprecation.

"And he released unto them him that for sedition and murder was cast into prison, whom they desired, but delivered Jesus to their will." "He was despised and rejected of men."

THE SCOURGING AND MOCKING.

"So Pilate, willing to content the people, released Barabbas unto them, and delivered Jesus, when he had scourged Him, to be crucified." Scourged Him! what does that mean? Not the chastisement allowed by the Mosaic code for minor offences, being forty stripes at the utmost,[1] but the Roman scourging, which was fearfully cruel. The victim was publicly stripped, was tied by the hands, in a bent position, to a pillar; then, on the naked back, he was beaten, not with a rod, but with leathern thongs, weighted with jagged fragments of bone and lead. Every blow brought blood, until the quivering

[1] Deut. xv. 3.

nerves were laid bare. Under the lacerating agony of this infliction the victim generally fainted, and oftentimes died.

Immediately after this terrific and exhausting infliction, Jesus is handed over to the scorn and contemptuous cruelty of the soldiers. These lead Him to the hall: they gather the whole band, a cohort, — being one-tenth of a legion,—and load Him with the most cruel mockery and insult. That the victim is a Jew, and is defenceless, only adds keenness to their brutal treatment. They dress Him as a fool. They strip off the white robe in which Herod had arrayed Him, now soaked with blood; they perform the ceremony of a mock inauguration. They throw over His shoulders a purple robe—a Roman military cloak; for a crown they plait a green wreath of thorns, and thrust it violently upon His head; for a sceptre, they put a reed in His tied hands. The robe, the crown of thorns, and the reed, were the mock emblems of the royalty which Jesus was accused of claiming. Then, with bended knee, they tauntingly cry, " Hail, King of the Jews!" Then, with contempt and scorn, they spit upon Him; they smite Him with their hands; they smite Him upon the head with the reed. So the prophetic words are fulfilled: "I gave My back to the smiters, and My cheeks to them that plucked off the hair: I hid not My face from shame and spitting."[1] "He giveth His cheek to him that smiteth Him: He is filled full with reproach."[2] Pilate, according to custom, was present, and witnessed the scourging and these acts of mockery and insult. Such treatment of a man whom he knew to be innocent, smote him, and stirred up the sense of justice and humanity, and thereupon he determined to make another effort to save Him from death.

"Pilate therefore went forth again, and saith unto them, Behold, I bring Him forth to you, that ye may know that I find no fault in Him." He may have said, I have tried Him by torture, and have failed to extort any confession. "I find no fault in Him." Hoping that the sight of Jesus might move their manly sympathy, he brought Him forth, saying, "Behold the Man." His face and hair and shoulders clotted with His blood; His

[1] Isa. l. 6.   [2] Lam. iii. 30.

face swollen with the blows of the soldiers, and His countenance marred with exhaustion and weariness,—"His visage so marred more than any man, and His form more than the sons of men!" Let His wretchedness plead with you. Has He not suffered enough? Save, oh, save Him from the ignominy and agonies of crucifixion!—In vain. There was no pity in the heart of the priests. Fearing that the people might be moved by this touching appeal, they waited not for them, but instantly "cried out, Crucify Him, Crucify Him!" Then, in irony and contempt, "Pilate saith unto them, Take ye Him, and crucify Him: for I find no fault in Him."

The priests now abandon for the time the political charge of sedition, and fall back upon the charge of blasphemy. "We have a law, and by our law He ought to die, because He made Himself the Son of God." "Cæsar is our master; still, he governs us by our laws. By our law, blasphemy merits death. And as we cannot execute Him by stoning, we demand that you should crucify this blasphemer."

This position nearly defeated their plan, by giving a new direction to the fears of Pilate, and leading him to renew his private examination of Jesus. According to Pilate's religion, it was consistent for the gods to appear among men. Barnabas and Paul were supposed by the people of Lystra to be Jupiter and Mercury. "When Pilate therefore heard that saying," "He made Himself the Son of God," "he was the more afraid." To crucify one of the gods or the son of the gods would be a monstrous iniquity. He "went again into the judgment hall, and saith unto Jesus, Whence art Thou?" What is thy real origin? Of what Father? Now perhaps the miracles of Jesus, of which he had heard, crowd upon his mind, and suggest to Pilate that superhuman powers may belong to Him. "Whence art Thou? But Jesus gave him no answer." It was too late to answer now: Pilate was too deeply committed. He was entangled in the toils of the priests. Jesus had been strictly examined, and again and again by Pilate pronounced innocent; and yet he had given Him up to His false accusers, knowing that for envy, and not for crime, they had delivered Him. Why should He make any reply?

"Then Pilate," if not with anger, certainly with surprise, "saith unto Him, Speakest Thou not unto *me*? knowest Thou not that I have power to crucify Thee, and have power to release Thee?" Yes, as an earthly judge thou hast the power of life and death. Why speak of that, and not of justice, and truth, and conscience, and rectitude? Power! "Thou couldest have no power at all against Me, except it were given thee from above." "It is not simply to Cæsar that you are accountable, but to God, whose Providence has placed My life in your hands. I know of your repeated declarations of My innocence, and of your desire to release Me. I know also your weakness, and your fear of the high priests and the outbreak of the people, and I pity you. To give Me up to crucifixion, knowing Me to be innocent, is indeed a crime, a very great crime. But yours is not the greatest guilt. Judas, and Annas, and Caiaphas, having better knowledge and greater strength of purpose, they are the most guilty."

"He that delivered me unto thee hath the

greater sin." This language shows deep compassion, and almost, if not quite, implies forgiveness. So impressed by it was Pilate that from thenceforth he " sought to release Him."

No sooner did he return to the priests and announce this determination, than he found that their malice was fertile in expedients; "the Jews cried out, saying, If thou let this man go, thou art not Cæsar's friend : whosoever maketh himself a king speaketh against Cæsar." Thus they appealed to Pilate's personal political interests. With a menacing air they told him that if he released Christ they would accuse him to the emperor as derelict in duty and conniving at treason.

This appeal to his official and political interests was more potent than every other consideration. It awakened fears on the other side, and shook his resolution to the foundation. Conscious of maladministration and tyranny in many things, he was frightened at the mere thought of being accused to the emperor. For awhile he buffeted the temptation. "When Pilate therefore heard that saying, he brought Jesus forth, and sat down in the judgment seat in a place that is called the Pavement, but in the Hebrew, Gabbatha:[1] ... and he saith unto the Jews, Behold your King!" He knew that they were expecting a king to arise, under whom they hoped to be freed from Roman bondage. To call this beaten, blood-stained, insulted sufferer their king, stirred the deepest dregs of their malice; and, with intensest contempt, they "cried out, Away with Him, away with Him, crucify Him!" Pilate, perhaps with taunting anger, "saith unto them, Shall I crucify your King?" With determined hatred the chief priests rejected Jesus, saying, "We have no king but Cæsar. Then delivered he Him therefore unto them to be crucified." Then, when they hedged him in with threats to bring him before the Emperor Tiberius; then, when his fears were alarmed lest he should lose his office; then, under the pressure of political interests, the deed was done, and "he delivered Him

---

[1] "Gabbatha (literally, the back), or the pavement, was a space between the Castle of Antonia and the western corner of the Temple, where the ridge of the rock or hill was paved with smooth stones. (Josephus, *Bell. Jud.* v. 5. 8.) Here, in full view of the Temple, and before the Jewish multitudes, Pilate took his place on the judgment seat, to deliver to death Jesus, though he held Him to be innocent."
—Robinson's *Harmony*.

unto them to be crucified. And they took Jesus, and led Him away."[1]

THE CRUCIFIXION.

The order being given to prepare the cross, the soldiers having again mocked Him, took off the purple military Roman toga and put on Him His own raiment. As no mention is made of the crown of thorns, it is most probable that He died wearing it, in derision of the title, "King of the Jews." "They took Jesus, and led Him away." "And He, bearing His cross [the tranverse beam], went forth into a place which is called in the Hebrew Golgotha." "The bodies of those beasts, whose blood is brought into the sanctuary by the high priest for sin, are burned without the camp. Wherefore Jesus also, that He might sanctify the people with His own blood, suffered with-

---

[1] "That Pilate sent some official account of the trial and crucifixion to Tiberius would be à priori probable, and seems to be all but certain (Justin Martyr, Apol. i. 76; Tertullian, Apol. 21; Eusebius, Hist. Eccl. ii. 2; Lardner, vi. 606); but it is equally certain that the existing Acta, Paradosis, Mors, and Epistolæ Pilati are spurious."—Farrar, Life of Christ, vol. ii. p. 392, note.

out the gate." [1] As He sinks under this burden, they "compel one Simon, a Cyrenian, the father of Alexander and Rufus, to bear His cross." Among the thronging company of people there were certain sympathising "women, who bewailed and lamented Him." Jesus, rising above His own troubles, gave this last warning of the miseries which awaited Jerusalem and the Jewish people: "Daughters of Jerusalem, weep not for Me," for this crucifixion is the end of all My sufferings; "but weep for yourselves, and for your children. For, behold, the days are coming, in the which they shall say, Blessed are the barren, and the wombs that never bare, and the paps which never gave suck." "Then," as predicted by the prophet Hosea,[2] "shall they begin to say to the mountains, Fall on us; and to the hills, Cover us." Thus, with death certain and speedy, He affirms His prediction of the judgment of Jerusalem, with all its terrific accompaniments. He confirms this solemn warning by the statement, that if they do the things now being done by cruel mockery and crucifixion,

[1] Heb. xiii. 11, 12.   [2] Hosea x. 8.

"in the green tree," lovely in its verdure, the symbol of His innocence and worth, "what shall be done in the dry?" which has filled up its measure and is no longer of use, the symbol of those who put the innocent Son of man to death, and imprecated His blood upon their own and children's heads. "Some of you, and certainly some of your children, will live to see that day. Weep not tears of sympathy for My sufferings, but weep penitential tears for yourselves, that ye may escape in the evil day." Compassionate, loving Saviour!

The soldiers, with the accompanying throng of people, moved along until they reached the place called Golgotha, or, in the Latin, Calvary, that is "a skull." There is no evidence that it was a hill or mount. The Scriptures simply call it "a place," probably the well-known place for public executions. As to its site there is no certain evidence. Robinson thinks it was a place on the side of some public road, near the city. Here they halted. "Then were there two thieves crucified with Him, one on the right hand, and another on the left." The selection of these criminals for execution at the same time may have been intended as a further mark of ignominy, or as evidence that the law regarded each as worthy of the same death. Thus " was He numbered with the transgressors." As a matter of humanity it was customary, immediately before crucifixion, to give to the condemned a draught of wine, medicated with some strong opiate, to reduce the consciousness of pain. " They gave Him to drink wine [a weak acid wine, the common drink of the soldiers], mingled with myrrh; but He received it not "—" He would not drink." He would meet His death in the full possession of His intellectual and moral power.

Crucifixion was not a Jewish but a Roman punishment. The cross consisted of a strong upright post, with a transverse beam a little below the top, also having a short bar or stake about the middle, which passed between the legs. On this bar the weight of the body principally rested. This, whilst it diminished the sufferings at first, made them much more lingering.

The cross being prepared, our Lord, being

stripped of His clothes, was laid at full length upon it. His arms were stretched along the transverse beam, and through each hand a strong iron spike was driven firmly into the wood. The legs were then drawn down at full length, and through each foot separately, or through both, placed one over the other, another spike tore its way through the bones and muscles and nerves and quivering flesh. It is believed that it was at this point of the process that the Divine Sufferer uttered that most wonderful and benevolent of all prayers, "FATHER, FORGIVE THEM, FOR THEY KNOW NOT WHAT THEY DO."

It was customary for the governor to put on the cross a writing signifying the crime of the victim. In the case of Jesus the writing was," JESUS OF NAZARETH, THE KING OF THE JEWS." This was written in the official Latin, in the usual Greek, and in the Hebrew, that all might know that this person, crucified between two thieves, was the "KING OF THE JEWS." This title was offensive to the chief priests, who desired Pilate so to change it as to read, "HE SAID, I AM the King of the Jews." Pilate answered, "What I have written, I have written." His motive may have had a political as well as a sarcastic tinge. You charged Him with sedition, making Himself the King of the Jews, and you appealed to my loyalty to Cæsar to crucify Him: I vindicate my loyalty, and I crucify Him as "the King of the Jews."

Then, with its "living human burden hanging upon it with helpless agony," the cross was raised by the soldiers to a perpendicular position, and made firm in the earth. The feet were raised only a little from the ground. Thus the sufferer was in the reach of any one disposed to smite, to mock, or in any other way to insult or torment Him.

Having erected the cross, the soldiers proceeded to divide among themselves His garments, "and made four parts, to every soldier a part." The coat, not being made of different pieces, but "without seam, woven from the top throughout," they would not rend, and thus make it useless, but determined to cast lots for it; thus fulfilling the prophecy, "They parted My raiment among them, and for My vesture they did cast lots."[1]

The arms being extended, and sustaining a part of the weight of the body, the least motion produced intense pain. The disturbed circulation of the blood, with its accumulation in the head and heart, became the source of inexpressible misery. The inflammation, arising from the exposure of the wounds to the air, and their constant irritation by the pressure of the nails, occasioned feverish excitement and intense thirst. Whilst enduring these bodily sufferings " they that passed by reviled Him, wagging their heads" in scornful insult. " The soldiers mocked Him, . . . offering Him vinegar, and saying, If Thou be the King of the Jews, save Thyself." The chief priests, with the scribes and elders, derided and mocked Him. " Let Christ, the King of Israel, descend now from the cross, that we may see and believe." Strange, though true, " the thieves cast the same in His teeth ;" they " railed on Him, saying, If Thou be Christ, save Thyself and us." What a chorus of scorn, derision, and malediction !

[1] Psa. xxii. 18. (Septuagint.)

This indeed was the hour and the power of darkness. "When reviled, He reviled not again." But the moment that one penitent tremulous word of petition was heard amid the tumultuous shoutings of scorn, it stirred His tenderest sympathies. One thief rebuked his fellow, saying, "Dost not thou fear God, seeing thou art in the same condemnation? And we indeed justly; for we receive the due reward of our deeds; but this man hath done nothing amiss." Who can tell what memories of a whole life, clear, distinct, and individual, with lightning speed, rushed through his mind? Who can tell how sorrow and condemnation lashed him with scorpion power, as each sin stood out fresh on the tablet of memory? Who can tell what sinkings of heart and utter despair overwhelmed him? Who can tell what long-neglected truth, or what he had heard or seen of Christ's miracles of mercy, now quicken his desire and hope? What the Holy Spirit did then and there no man knoweth. But the Lord Jesus knew all. He saw in the thief real penitence and faith. The thief confessed and condemned his sins;

he acknowledged the justice of and accepted the penalty of his guilt. He avowed his confidence in the innocency of Christ, and that He was the true Messiah. Then the simple, touching, confiding prayer, "Lord, remember me when Thou comest into Thy kingdom."

This prayer of faith so appealed to the wondrous love of Christ that it brought an immediate and assuring answer: "This day shalt thou be with Me in paradise."

Now the sun itself withdrew its light, and held back every cheering beam. "From the sixth hour there was darkness over all the land unto the ninth hour." Pain and sorrow has a double power when endured in the silent lone hours of darkness. How the sufferer longs for the break of day! The light of heaven, though not curative, still relieves the heavy pressure and makes the pain and the sorrow more endurable. But here there was darkness, unnatural darkness—gloom, supernatural and terrific. It continued through all the unutterable anguish which drank up the life, and which rolled in heavy surges over the soul of the Redeemer. He suffered and died in those dark hours.¹ *Here Christianity was born.* Bright hours come out of the darkness. "Weeping may endure for a night, but joy cometh in the morning." The angels the holy angels, the ready attendants upon His will, the angel who announced His conception, the angels who at His birth sang heavenly music, the angels charged "to keep Him, and in their hands to bear Him up," and who ministered unto Him after His long fasting and severe temptations of the devil, and who strengthened Him after His agony in the garden, drew back. When He hung upon the cross they were not there. In this hour of His deepest sorrow, when all was dark, and the fierce powers of hell were in revelry, then, when forsaken by His disciples, forsaken by the sun in the heavens, then not an angel stood by. The Sufferer was

---

[1] "And it was about the sixth hour, and there was darkness over all the earth until the ninth hour. And the sun was darkened." "The early Fathers," writes Dr. Farrar, "appealed to pagan authorities—the historian Phallus, the chronicler Phlegon—for such a darkness; but we have no means of testing the accuracy of these references, and it is quite possible that the darkness was a local gloom which hung densely over the guilty city and its immediate neighbourhood."—*Life of Christ*, vol. ii. p. 414.

all alone! This was not the worst; the deepest depth was the forsaking of His Father. His Heavenly Father then forsook Him. Oh, the measureless anguish of that piteous cry, "My God! My God! why hast Thou forsaken Me?" All the bodily sufferings, all the scoffings and insults, all the shutting out of the light of heaven, all the desertion of men and angels, He could bear, had borne, without one word of complaint; but, oh, when His Father, His God, forsook Him, then He was filled with heaviness; then His soul was exceeding sorrowful even unto death; then grief came with such withering, crushing power that He could bear up no longer. But, with holy submission and unwavering confidence, "He cried with a loud voice, Father, into Thy hands I commend My spirit;" "IT IS FINISHED;" then His swollen heart burst; "He bowed His head;" "He gave up the ghost." *He died all alone.*

Blessed Jesus! the bowing of Thy head was death indeed,—death such as none other could die. The shedding of Thy blood was the offering of atonement for the sins of the world.

One touching incident shines out amid the gloom. "Now there stood by the cross of Jesus His mother." During the long weary hours of sorrow and anguish, the mother and the beloved disciple had urged their way up very near to the cross. When Jesus saw them standing by, tenderly and sadly He thought of the future that awaited her. He knew that fierce tumults and persecutions would gather up their strength to crush His cause. As He could make no gesture with His hands, nailed as they were to the cross, He bent His head, and with the utmost tenderness and affection said, "*Woman, behold thy son;*" and to John, "*Behold thy mother.*" They caught these words of love, this dying legacy. The legacy was promptly accepted. From that hour—peradventure from that moment—John led her away, that her motherly heart might not be rent with unavailing agony as the cruel work of crucifixion passed on into increasingly intense sufferings. "And from that hour that disciple took her to his own home." Jesus committed His mother, then most probably a widow, not to Joseph of Arimathæa, a rich and honourable councillor, "a disciple, but secretly for fear of the Jews;" not to Nicodemus, a rich member of the Sanhedrim, who acknowledged Christ "as a teacher come from God;" not to His own brethren, who did not **believe in Him,**[1] but **He gave her to** John, an avowed disciple. Though possibly **poor** in this world's goods and honours, He knew that John would stand by her through all perils.

Other warm but sorrowing hearts were **witnesses of** His death. "Many women were there beholding afar off, which followed Jesus from Galilee, ministering unto Him: among whom was Mary Magdalene, and **Mary** the mother of James and Joses, and **the mother** of Zebedee's children."

Brave, loving women!

> "**Not she with** traitorous kiss the Saviour stung,
> Not she denied Him with unholy tongue,
> **She,** when apostles shrank, could dangers brave :
> **Last** at the **cross,** and earliest at the grave."

The Lord expired at the ninth hour, answering to our three o'clock **in the** afternoon, when the evening sacrifice was being offered **in** the Temple, when the priest would be

[1] John vii. 5.

burning incense in the holy place, whilst the people were praying without. It was at this critical moment that the veil of the Temple, by unseen hands, was rent, not upwards from the bottom, as could easily have been done, but from the top downwards, high up, beyond unaided human reach. This miraculous rending of the veil, accompanied, as it doubtless was, with the sound of tearing its thick fabric, must have attracted the notice of the attending priests, and filled them with awe and terror, as it laid open to vulgar gaze the Holy of Holies, into which alone the high priest was permitted to enter but once a year, and that the day of atonement.

Simultaneous with, or hard upon it, the deep foundations of the earth were shaken; the tombs of the dead were burst open; a wild consternation seized all the people, who, in their terror, smote their breasts. "The centurion and they that were with him feared greatly."

This rending of the veil of the Temple was not a mere incident: it indicated that the time had come when the restricted exclusiveness of the Jewish typical dispensation had come to an end: it prefigured "the entering of Christ, as the high priest of His people, into the presence of His Father, there to present the atonement He had made for their sins." "For Christ is not entered into the holy places made with hands, which are the figures of the true; but into heaven itself, now to appear in the presence of God for us."[1] This rending further denotes the removal of all restrictions, and that access to God is now free and open to all: "Having therefore, brethren, boldness to enter into the holiest by the blood of Jesus, by a new and living way, which He hath consecrated for us, through the veil, that is to say, His flesh."[2]

We have now another illustration of the punctiliousness with which the high priests and scribes adhered to ceremonial observances whilst hardening their hearts against all mercy, and consummating the murder of an innocent man.

"The Jews therefore, because it was the preparation, that the bodies should not remain upon the cross on the sabbath day, (for that sabbath day was an high day,) besought Pilate

[1] Heb. ix. 24. [2] Heb. x. 19, 20.

that their legs might be broken, and that they might be taken away." The design of this was to hasten death. In obedience to the orders of Pilate, the soldiers broke the legs of the two thieves. "But when they came to Jesus, and saw that He was dead already, they brake not His legs: but one of the soldiers," either through wanton cruelty or to secure the actual death, "with a spear pierced His side, and forthwith came there out blood and water." By these peculiar incidents these soldiers unwittingly fulfilled two remarkable predictions: "A bone of Him shall not be broken;" "They shall look on Him whom they pierced." They also established beyond all doubt the fact that Jesus had really died. The decomposed blood—the result, in all probability, of mental agony, and the sign of a literally "broken heart"[1]—made it impossible to maintain, with any show of truth, as some have ventured to assert, that our Lord was only in a swoon—the semblance of death—when taken from the cross. On the profound interpreta-

[1] See Dr. Stroud. *Inquiry into the Physical Cause of the Death of Christ*

tion of the symbol, as given by the beloved disciple,[1] we cannot enter now. Enough to say that it represented the *sacrifice* and the *purification*, which were the two great realities of Calvary.

[1] See 1 John v. 6.

X.

THE BURIAL.

CHAPTER X.

THE BURIAL.

THAT Christ was actually dead admits of no serious doubt. That "Pilate marvelled if He were already dead" does not sanction the surmise of some, that it was only a seeming death, a fainting fit, a syncope, a temporary suspension of the animal functions. Recall the facts attendant upon His arrest. He was seized and bound with cords, and hurried away to Annas, then to Caiaphas. He was compelled to stand the whole time of His trial. He was faint from the want of food and the loss of blood from scourging. During these long-continued exhausting hours there were no alleviations, no intervals for quietude and rest, and no opportunity for sleep. From the moment when they seized Him, by night and by day, with unrelenting perseverance, they crowded Him on until they nailed Him to the cross. What He suffered whilst hanging there no mortal mind can conceive. The mental agony and soul travail in the garden so exhausted His humanity that an angel was sent to strengthen Him. No wonder, when forsaken by His Father, and no strengthening angel near, that He bowed His head and gave up the ghost. The wonder is, not that He died so soon, but that He endured so long. Pilate was satisfied that He was dead.

Among those who witnessed the execution was Joseph of Arimathæa, a man distinguished for his birth, wealth, and office. He was a native of Arimathæa, in the territory of Benjamin, on the mountain range of Ephraim, not far from Gibeah. His residence was either in Jerusalem or its vicinity. He is described as an "honourable counsellor." It is the opinion of the learned Macknight, that he was one of the council of Pilate, who aided him in managing the affairs of the province, and was personally and intimately acquainted with the governor.

He was also a member of the Sanhedrim, for it is particularly recorded " the same had not consented to the counsel and deed of them," the Sanhedrim, to put Christ to death. It is also stated that he was a " good man, and just," who " waited for the kingdom of God," " being a disciple of Jesus, but secretly for fear of the Jews." Though convinced, from his knowledge of the prophets, and the manifested works and teachings of Jesus, that He was the Messiah, still, through timidity or imagined prudence, his convictions were kept in abeyance by the malignant attitude of the rulers. He was not yet prepared to meet the peril of excommunication. But the strange scenes which he had witnessed deeply moved him. His sorrow and his indignation inspired him with unwonted courage. Such were the natural causes of his resolve. But we doubt not that the Spirit of God, with persuasive power, touched his heart and nerved him to resolute action. Now his love for Jesus is stronger than his fear of the Jews. He knew that the body of his Lord, if it were treated as those of malefactors generally, would either be buried at the foot of the cross on which He died, or would be hurried to the potter's field, and there consigned to a dishonoured grave; or, when the flesh was removed and consumed, the bones, and only the bones, would be deposited in the ancestral tomb. To prevent this ignominy, he " came and went in boldly unto Pilate and craved," " begged," " besought " the " body of Jesus." These strong expressions show the intensity of his purpose. Had Peter or John, or any one, or all, of the known disciples, made this request, Pilate, aware of the feelings and suspicions of the rulers of the Jews, might not have consented. But when Joseph, his personal friend and a counsellor, and known to all as a man of wealth and station, a " good man, and just," incapable of any intrigue or dishonourable conduct, craved the body, he granted the request.

Joseph, when he had taken down the body from the cross, "bought fine linen," "and wrapped the body in the linen." The body, being washed, was wrapped in a sheet, then it was swathed with long bandages of linen, a few inches wide, tightly around the body.

Thus prepared, Joseph laid the body "in his own new tomb, which he had hewn out in the rock," "wherein never man before was laid," "and rolled a great stone to the door of the sepulchre, and departed." These few facts illustrate the characteristics of Joseph. He was just, but cautious; honourable, but fearful; loving, but timid; yet when the circumstances demanded, his sense of justice and honour, under the control of love, over-rode his timidity, fear, and caution, and made him bold, resolute, and courageous.

Nicodemus also was a witness of the execution. He was a Pharisee, and a member of the Sanhedrim. He too was timid and cautious, and not forward to commit himself to an unpopular cause. He had manifested candour, and a desire for instruction, when he came to Jesus by night, saying, "Rabbi, we know that Thou art a teacher come from God: for no man can do these miracles that Thou doest, except God be with him." He had stood up for Christ before the Sanhedrim, saying, "Doth our law judge any man before it hear him, and know what he doeth?" The boldness and unreserve of

Joseph, whose previous sentiments he knew, awakened a kindred feeling. "There came also Nicodemus . . . and brought a mixture of myrrh and aloes, about an hundred pound weight." "Then took they the body of Jesus, and wound it in linen clothes with the spices, as the manner of the Jews is to bury." Thus, though Christ "died like a malefactor, He was buried like a king." Love so wrought in Nicodemus as to conquer his selfish fear, and, in this most trying hour, when the malignant hatred of the rulers had secured the death of Christ, it drew him forth into open and avowed discipleship. Where there is true love, such is its nature that it must manifest itself. The Providence of God will also so appeal to it as certainly to call it forth, no matter how forbidding may be the surrounding circumstances. Thus it was with Joseph and Nicodemus; and they but illustrate what is often seen. For though love to Christ may be feeble in its beginnings, and in conflict with opposing selfish influences, still it will grow and strengthen, and overcome all other powers, and assert and maintain its supremacy. In the Providence of God these honourable and just men were held back until the fitting opportunity should arrive, when their personal services were indispensable. Thus God brought good out of the evil of secret discipleship. Thus the body of Christ was so placed as to secure its whereabouts and its identity, that the proofs of its resurrection might be clear and indisputable.

The jealous vigilance of the Jewish rulers eagerly noticed all these movements of Joseph and Nicodemus; and that no opportunity might be afforded for removing the body from the tomb, "the chief priests and Pharisees came together unto Pilate, saying, Sir, we remember that that deceiver said, while He was yet alive, After three days I will rise again. Command therefore that the sepulchre be made sure until the third day, lest His disciples come by night, and steal Him away, and say unto the people, He is risen from the dead: so the last error shall be worse than the first. Pilate said unto them, Ye have a watch: go your way, make it as sure as ye can. So they went, and made the sepulchre sure, sealing the stone, and setting a watch." Thus, under the wise arrangement of Providence, both love and wrath, both friend and enemy, united to guard the body and render the proof of the resurrection grand and triumphant.

THE WOMEN.

Loving women were there, and attended the funeral. "Now there stood by the cross of Jesus His mother, and His mother's sister, Mary the wife of Cleophas, and Mary Magdalene." "And many women were there, beholding afar off, which followed Jesus from Galilee."

First stands the VIRGIN MOTHER, who, beyond all parallel, was the most interested and distinguished mourner. She did not stand "beholding afar off." She urged her way forward until she stood near, very near, the cross, so near that she could watch the beating of His labouring heart and hear the deep breathings of His heaving breast. She read the tender sympathy of His loving eyes as they turned upon her. She treasured the last words He ever spoke to her: "Woman, behold thy son!" "Behold thy mother!"

She could bear no more: the mother's heart was full; her sorrow was too deep for words, too deep for tears. "And from that hour that disciple took her to his own home." They moved away. But the Sufferer endured until all was finished, then He gave up the ghost.

MARY MAGDALENE is so named from the place of her birth or residence, and perhaps to distinguish her from the other Marys. She had been afflicted with a demoniacal possession: "Out of whom went seven devils." The number seven is the symbol of perfection, and here denotes the entireness and severity of the possession, rather than the number of devils. The casting out of seven devils from Mary Magdalene is no more a proof that she was a dissolute and impure character, than does the casting out of the devil from the daughter of the Syrophenician woman prove that this maiden was a prostitute. The too common belief that Mary Magdalene was a woman of unchaste character has no foundation in the Scriptures. It rests only on vague tradition, which the best of the early Fathers rejected.

This Mary has been strangely confounded

with "the woman" who is called "a sinner," who anointed the feet of Jesus.[1] There are but two occasions on which the feet of Christ were anointed. In neither of these are we told that Mary Magdalene took any part. The first occurred in the house of a Pharisee, perhaps in Capernaum, where "a woman in the city, which was a sinner . . . brought an alabaster box of ointment," and anointed His feet. So well known was her character that the Pharisee who had invited Christ to eat with him was shocked that the Lord allowed this fallen and polluted woman to touch Him. The Lord the rather confirmed this view of her character when He said, " Her sins, which are many, are forgiven ; for she loved much." Here are sins forgiven, but no intimation of devils cast out. This unnamed woman appears to have been a resident of Capernaum; but Mary was of Magdala, on the shore of Gennesaret.

The second anointing took place at " Bethany, in the house of Simon the leper," when Mary, the sister of Martha and Lazarus, anointed the feet of Jesus. The incidents of

[1] Luke vii. 37.

this latter case much resemble those named of the woman who "was a sinner." The difference, however, in time and place forbid that these can be identical.

How, then, stands the evidence? Luke vii. 37 tells of a fallen woman of Capernaum, whose name is not given, but whose many sins the Saviour forgave. Subsequently, chap. viii. 2, Luke makes mention of "certain women, which had been healed of evil spirits and infirmities," and gives prominence to "Mary called Magdalene, out of whom went seven devils." The record further says that Mary Magdalene, in company with "Joanna the wife of Chuza Herod's steward, and Susanna, and many others," ministered unto Christ of their substance. I think I am warranted in saying there is not the slightest trustworthy evidence that Mary Magdalene was ever a loose, abandoned woman. On the other hand, there is evidence that she was a lady of property and station. Having experienced healing mercies at the hands of Christ, she gratefully devoted herself and her wealth to His service. All the subsequent references to her are most commendable. After ministering to Jesus in Galilee, she accompanied Him from Galilee to Jerusalem on His last visit to the Temple. She was with Him at His death, and as near to the cross as the Roman troops and the thronging crowds would permit. She was present at His burial, " and beheld where He was laid." She was early at the tomb on the morning of the third day, and a prominent actor amid the stirring scenes of the resurrection. In all that is recorded of her the evidence is clear that she was affectionate, generous, exemplary, and courageous. Her resolute spirit gave her prominence. This may be the reason why some of the evangelists mention only this Mary when it is evident that other women were present. Religion did not change her natural temperament, but gave shape and direction to it. Her love and her courage stand out without a cloud. There is nothing certain in tradition as to her subsequent activity, or the time, manner, and place of her death. We cannot doubt that she filled up her days with loving cheerful service, and that, through grace, she had a glorious welcome to the presence of her Lord.

MARY, THE WIFE OF CLEOPHAS, being the sister of the Virgin Mother, her sons, viz. James the Less, Simon, Joses, and Judas (not Iscariot), were cousins to the Saviour, and, according to Hebrew usage, were called his brethren.[1] She was one of the women who followed Christ and ministered unto Him. She was present at the crucifixion, followed the body to the sepulchre, and sat disconsolate at the tomb. These few glimpses are enough to develop her real character. She was true-hearted and affectionate. Her courage was quiet, but invincible. Not so energetic and enterprising, perhaps, as Mary Magdalene, she was as enduring and unwearied in her devotion to Christ. We have no record or tradition of her subsequent life and death. But what inspiration has written of her is so bright and decided that no shadow of doubt clouds her career.

SALOME is called the mother of Zebedee's children, viz. James the Elder, and John the

---

[1] Such is the conclusion which I have been led to adopt on a difficult question. Into other theories respecting the "brethren" of Jesus, or into the question whether Mary the wife of Cleophas (Clopas) was different from the sister of the Virgin (John xix. 25), this is not the place to enter.

evangelist. She was one of the women "who followed Jesus from Galilee, ministering unto Him." She was at the crucifixion, and at the burial, and "beheld where they laid Him." Before His death and resurrection, she had mistaken views of the nature of Christ's kingdom, and her ambition for the advancement of her sons cropped out when she asked that "one might sit on His right hand, and the other on His left." Still, she was stedfast in her devotion, and in the most trying scenes her love was strong and unfaltering. She has a good record, and doubtless finished her course with joy.

The above are all who are mentioned by name; "many others" who had come up with Him to Jerusalem had witnessed His death, and no doubt took part in His sepulture. Their " names are written in heaven ! "

But with the shade of that sad evening the Sabbath had begun. These brave and loving ones must rest awhile, " according to the commandment," before they could complete the mournful last offices to which affection clings. But, courage ! The weary hours pass, and THE MORNING COMETH.

XI.

THE RESURRECTION.

CHAPTER XI.

THE RESURRECTION.[1]

DURING the interval between the going down of the sun on Friday and the rising of the same on the first day of the week, the most important of events occurred. It was the RESURRECTION of CHRIST. It was seen by no human eye. How it was accomplished is not stated. Perhaps the angels, who had a special charge concerning His

---

[1] Students of the Bible find it difficult to harmonise, with perfect accuracy, all the incidents connected with the resurrection of Christ as they are recorded by the different evangelists. Without entering into the discussion of that subject, it is sufficient to say that, after much reflection, I have followed substantially the order laid down by Professor Edward Robinson, D.D., LL.D., in his *Harmony of the Four Gospels*. As far as practicable, I have given the incidents in the exact language of the evangelists, with such remarks as seemed called for to elucidate the narrative.

earthly mission, and who often ministered unto Him, were the Divinely-appointed agents. But the more probable, if not the certain solution is, that He arose by His own power. Did He not say, when speaking of His body, "Destroy this temple, and in three days I will raise it up?" and, again, "I lay down My life, that I might take it again. I have power to lay it down, and I have power to take it again?" Only some of the attendant circumstances are recorded, whilst the evidences of the fact are numerous and complete. "There was a great earthquake: for the angel of the Lord descended from heaven, and came and rolled back the stone from the door, and sat upon it. His countenance was like lightning, and his raiment white as snow: and for fear of him the keepers did shake, and became as dead men." Soon after this earthquake, and the descent of the angel to roll away the stone, the women came and found the tomb empty. From these facts it is clear that the resurrection took place before the early dawn. The Lord was laid in the sepulchre before sunset on Friday. He rose in the night, between the sundown of Saturday and the early dawn of Sunday. Thus the time He lay in the tomb could not be less than thirty-six or forty hours, and this met the oft-repeated prediction, "And the third day He shall rise again."[1]

THE VISIT TO THE SEPULCHRE.

It was strange to see several lone women, in the early morning twilight of the first day of the week, going forth from Jerusalem, to seek a tomb in a secluded garden. This tomb, they knew, was guarded with exacting vigilance by Roman soldiers. In it lay the body of a man recently crucified,—one whose life, and especially whose death, had intensely stirred the wonder and apprehension of all in the Holy City. These women had been witnesses of the strange and fearful sights which convulsed the whole population with fear. They had felt that unnatural darkness which, from "the sixth to the ninth hour," like the pall of death, spread "over all the land." They had heard the mutterings of the earthquake. They had felt the solid earth tremble and reel under

[1] Matt. xx. 19 ; Mark x. 34.

their feet. They had heard the rending of rocks, and the wild and piercing cry from the sanctuary, " The vail of the temple is rent in twain from the top to the bottom." Amidst all these terrible scenes they had heard the Sufferer, "with a loud voice, cry, My God, My God, why hast Thou forsaken Me?" "Father, into Thy hands I commend My spirit;" "It is finished." Then, in that dark hour of deep and awful silence, they saw Him bow His head in death. The centurion "feared greatly," and said, "Truly this was the Son of God." "And all the people that came together to that sight, beholding the things which were done, smote their breasts and returned." Through all these strange scenes of terror those women had stood firm. Though sorrow and anguish tore their hearts, they deserted Him not; they stedfastly looked on, and witnessed His death.

Their hearts were comforted when they saw Joseph of Arimathæa and Nicodemus take the body down from the cross, wrap it in fine linen with spices, and lay it in a " new tomb, hewn out from a rock, wherein never man was laid," and roll to the entrance a great stone. They "beheld the sepulchre, and how his body was laid." This was not that insatiable curiosity which impudently and irreverently crowds forward to unwelcome places. No, no: it was a personal affectionate concern that the body of their Lord should receive due respect in its burial. Having done all that they then could, and as the sun was nearing the western horizon, "they returned, and bought sweet spices and ointments; and rested the sabbath day, according to the commandment;" "for that Sabbath was an high day," being at once a Sabbath and a Passover.

"And when the Sabbath was past, Mary Magdalene, and Mary the mother of James, and Salome, had bought sweet spices, that they might come and anoint Him." As they had rested on the Sabbath, "according to the commandment," this purchase was probably made after sunset. The requisite preparation of the material for the completed burial took place during the evening, and perhaps far into the night.

"In the end of the Sabbath, as it began to dawn toward the first day of the week, came

Mary Magdalene and the other Mary to see the sepulchre." "And very early in the morning the first day of the week, they came unto the sepulchre at the rising of the sun." "The first day of the week cometh Mary Magdalene early, when it was yet dark, unto the sepulchre." All agree that the visit of these women to the tomb was on the first day of the week, and that it was "very early in the morning," "as it began to dawn," "when it was yet dark:" clearly intimating that it was in the very early twilight.

The mission of these women was one of love. On their way, as they talked together of the strange events which so terrified the whole city, they remembered the fact that a heavy stone had been rolled up to close the tomb; and "they said among themselves, Who shall roll us away the stone from the door of the sepulchre?" On this it is supposed that Mary Magdalene, with her characteristic energy and courage, ran ahead, and, arriving at the tomb, was amazed and filled with consternation when she found that the stone had been rolled away. Deeper still was her consternation—nay, her agony, when, on entering, she found not the body. Supposing that it had been removed, "she runneth, and cometh to Simon Peter, and to the other disciple, whom Jesus loved, and saith unto them, They have taken away the Lord out of the sepulchre, and we know not where they have laid Him."

The other women, when they arrived, "entering the sepulchre," saw one who is variously described as "an angel," or messenger, and " a young man, sitting on the right side, clothed in a long white garment." " As they were much perplexed thereabout, behold, two men stood by them in shining garments." Here is a striking illustration of how differently the same thing appears to different persons, viewed either from different standpoints or under different states of mind. All, however, agree that a Divine messenger said unto them, "Fear not ye;" "Be not affrighted: Ye seek Jesus of Nazareth, which was crucified:" "Why seek ye the living among the dead? He is not here, but is risen: Come, see the place where the Lord lay." Being thus quieted, comforted, and assured, for they now "remembered His words," the messenger bade them "go quickly, and tell His disciples that He is risen from the dead." "And they departed quickly from the sepulchre, with fear and great joy; and did run to bring His disciples word." While thus hastening to bear this joyful intelligence, "behold, Jesus met them, saysaying, All hail. And they came and held Him by the feet, and worshipped Him. Then said Jesus unto them, Be not afraid : go tell My brethren that they go into Galilee, and there shall they see Me."

When the women returned from the sepulchre, and told to the disciples all that they knew, "their words seemed to them as idle tales, and they believed them not." The disciples were then in a very despondent state of mind. They had certainly seen their Lord crucified, and actually buried, and his tomb guarded by Roman soldiers. They knew of the wrathful vigilance and the unconquerable hatred of the Jewish rulers; and how could it be that these women had actually seen Jesus alive again? In their perplexity and fear, these women must have been deceived. True, they knew that Jesus had brought back to life the daughter of Jairus, and the only son of the widow of Nain, and Lazarus also, who had been dead four days; but then Christ had miraculous powers from heaven. But now that *He* is dead, who is to raise *Him* from the grave? It has never yet been known that a dead man raised himself to life; and how can it be that Christ is alive? Alas, how strange that they did not cherish, with intense strength and confidence, His oft-repeated assurance that He would rise on the third day! Had they hidden these promises in their hearts, they would not have been despondent and unbelieving. The tidings of the women would not have seemed "as idle tales," but words of truth, the confirmation of Christ's own words; and with gladness and great joy they would have hastened to the appointed place of meeting in Galilee, that there they might see Him.

We must not judge them with severity, for they were but men, and were placed in circumstances unparalleled. Such strange and terrible things had never before concentrated in so short a space of time. All without them was wild and terrific. Wrath and clamour and murder swayed the masses, driven on by the unrelenting malice of the Jewish rulers. The forces of nature were convulsed; the earth quaking, the rocks rending, the graves opening, the sun like blood, the darkness at noon dense, deep, awful. Dread and terror, in their crushing power, paled every cheek and curdled the blood in every heart. Whichever way they looked, no kind eye met theirs; no response of sympathy met their appeals. They were shut up to themselves, as by encircling walls of adamant. In all the world around them there was no response to their sorrow. They had sorrow: their Lord, whom they loved and trusted, was dead; their hopes were dead; their plans were dead; all was desolation. Under these conditions it is not strange that the words of the women that He was alive " seemed to them as idle tales, and they believed them not." The news was too good to be true. Unbelief on this one point was not unnatural. So, when Peter was released from prison, in answer to the prayer which " was made without ceasing of the church unto God for him," and went "to the house of Mary, where many were gathered together praying," and "knocked at the gate," and "Rhoda, when she knew Peter's voice, opened not the gate for gladness,"—joy so sudden and unexpected having disturbed her judgment,— "she ran in," and told the praying circle "that Peter stood at the door." Did they believe her? Nay, they said, "Thou art mad." When "she constantly affirmed" that Peter was there, "they said, It is his angel." They would not believe in the answer to their own prayers until Peter, who "continued knocking," stood before them and spake unto them. Then seeing was believing. I think the disciples to whom the women carried the news of the resurrection of Christ were far more excusable for their unbelief in that fact than were these praying disciples for their unbelief in the release of Peter.

PETER AND JOHN.

Mary Magdalene found Peter and John, and told them that the tomb was open and the body was not there. This so stirred and roused them that "they ran both together:

and the other disciple did outrun Peter, and came first to the sepulchre. And he stooping down, and looking in, saw the linen clothes lying; yet went he not in. Then cometh Simon Peter following him, and went into the sepulchre, and seeth the linen clothes lie, and the napkin, that was about His head, not lying with the linen clothes, but wrapped together in a place by itself. Then went in also that other disciple, which came first to the sepulchre, and he saw, and believed." *Believed what?* Not that the body was gone. This he knew before, from the report of Mary Magdalene and the vacant tomb. He believed in the actual resurrection. The process by which he reached this conviction was simple and demonstrative. The napkin, "wrapped together in a place by itself," was a small, very small, item, one which by most would have been overlooked; but to his logical mind it poured in a flood of resistless evidence, which permanently settled his belief that Christ had actually risen from the dead. He knew that things small in human estimation played a conspicuous and essential part in the wonderful workings of Divine providence. The murderer, who, alone and in the most secret manner, executes his foul purpose, is detected and identified by some little thing which he could not have anticipated. Or by some trivial circumstance the most satisfactory proof of the innocence of an accused person is made evident. In like manner, the placing of this napkin relieved the mind of John from all the suspicions which may have disturbed it. He saw at once that the other disciples had not taken away the body while the soldiers slept. He came to this conclusion, not simply from his confidence in his fellow-disciples that they would neither steal nor fabricate a falsehood; nor from the fact that the disciples were in no mood for such a perilous enterprise; nor from the fact that he knew of their whereabouts during all that sorrowful night; but from the position of the napkin. Had the disciples taken away the body, they would not have stripped it, but would have hurried away with it, with all the linen clothes. Or, if anything had been dropped, in the hurry of so perilous an enterprise, it would have been loosely, carelessly placed where it fell.

It would be inconceivable that the disciples should pause to "wrap together" the napkin, and to lay it "in a place by itself."

He perceived, again, that the body had not been stolen by thieves, for the sake of gain. Such a supposition might naturally have been entertained by him on his way to the tomb. He knew that many thousands of strangers were at that season gathered to Jerusalem from all parts of the country, and that among these doubtless there were dishonest, unscrupulous men. Such, having heard of the munificence of Joseph and Nicodemus in the burial of the convict crucified, might determine in the night to rob the tomb of its treasures. But the moment he saw the "napkin wrapped together in a place by itself" he knew with absolute certainty that no robber band had entered the sepulchre. For had they come, they would have either stripped the body and carried away the linen and the spices, or they would have carried away the body as enveloped in the linen with the spices. But he saw that only the body was gone, whilst all the burial garments were left. This was not all, for he saw that the grave clothes were so arranged as to demonstrate that there had been neither haste nor confusion, but deliberation and order. " He saw, and believed," that the Saviour had actually risen from the grave.

How diverse, yet characteristic, was the action of these two apostles! Both were actuated by the same motive. So intense was that motive that both ran with their utmost speed. John reached the sepulchre first, and, stooping down, looked in and "saw the linen clothes lying," but saw no corpse there. Peter rushed up and fearlessly entered the tomb. He, too, saw "the linen clothes lie, and the napkin, that was about His head, not lying with the linen clothes, but wrapped together in a place by itself." He saw and wondered, but found no solution to the mystery of the disappearance of the body. Now John enters, and, fastening his searching eye upon the clothes as they lay, he immediately solved the difficulty. His conviction was vivid and settled. There, in that tomb, his heart palpitated with joy, for he knew of a certainty that the Lord, according to His promise, had risen on this the third day. This conviction John doubtless explained to Peter, "wondering in himself at that which was come to pass." "Then the disciples went away again unto their own home."

Mary Magdalene did not reach the sepulchre again until after Peter and John had left for their homes. She "stood without, weeping." Evidently she had not seen Peter and John, who would have told her of their belief in the resurrection. This would have dried up her tears. Her weeping was evidence not simply of her affection, but also that no thought that Christ had risen had yet entered her mind. "As she wept, she stooped down, and looked into the sepulchre." Her eyes followed her heart. The last she saw of Him was lying in that tomb. But where, alas where, is now that precious body? Her full burdened heart filled her eyes with tears of sorrow. Yet she could not keep her eyes away from the sepulchre; but, looking in, she "seeth two angels in white sitting, the one at the head, and the other at the feet, where the body of Jesus had lain. And they say unto her, Woman, why weepest thou?

She saith unto them, Because they have taken away my Lord, and I know not where they have laid Him." Her loving, faithful watching was richly rewarded. Scarcely had she ended her reply to the angels when she turned herself back, and saw Jesus standing, yet knew not that it was Jesus. Perhaps her eyes were dim with tears, or the morning mists still hung around; or she did not care to look with any attention to one whom she supposed a stranger; or *her eyes were holden*, like those of the travellers to Emmaus, later in the day. Jesus saith unto her, "Woman, why weepest thou?" Still firmly believing that the body of Christ had by unknown hands been carried away, she, "supposing Him to be the gardener," perhaps from His dress being different from what the soldiers divided, "saith unto Him, Sir, if Thou hast borne Him hence, tell me where Thou hast laid Him, and I will take Him away." She was intent upon finding the body, that it might receive the care which affection prompted. Nor did she stay to ask how she could bear the precious burden. "*I* will take Him away."

"Jesus saith unto her, Mary!" That tone thrilled along every nerve, and wakened up her whole soul to expectation. That look, gracious, tender, and full of affection, told all, and she knew Him; she knew He had risen, and, with the strongest words of reverence, saith unto Him, "Rabboni, Master." And in her humility she prostrated herself at His feet that she might embrace them. This He forbade: "Touch Me not"—cling not now to Me; for the time of full communion between My disciples and Myself has "not yet" come.

> "Touch Me not; awhile believe Me;
> Touch Me not, till heaven receive Me;
> Then draw near, and never leave Me;
> Then I go no more."[1]

The commission was then given to Mary to tell the disciples—Christ's "brethren"—that He was about to ascend to His Father and their Father, to His God and their God! He has achieved their redemption, and now He and they are eternally one! Immediately she returned to the city, and told the disciples that she had seen the risen Lord.

[1] Keble.

THE TESTIMONY OF THE SOLDIERS.

As the women were returning to Jerusalem, "some of the watch came into the city, and showed unto the chief priests all the things that were done." That is, they told of the earthquake, "that an angel of the Lord had descended from heaven," "whose countenance was like lightning, and his raiment white as snow;" that he came and rolled back the stone from the door, and sat upon it, and that, for fear of him, they, the keepers, did shake and became as dead men. This is a plain, intelligible, straightforward story. It implies, though it does not distinctly assert, that the body was gone. For if the body was still in the tomb, there could be no cause for anxiety. The chief priests understood that the body had disappeared. This the people would regard as the fulfilment of His prediction, "After three days I will rise again." The disappearance must be accounted for. The Sanhedrim are convened. "And when they were assembled with the elders, and had taken counsel, they gave large money unto the soldiers, saying, Say ye, His disciples came by night, and stole Him away while we slept." The soldiers had a serious difficulty in the way of accepting the money with the condition attached. It was death for a Roman soldier to sleep upon his post. This difficulty was overcome by the assurance that " if this come to the governor's ears, we will persuade him, and secure you." Three things are here stated as facts, viz. that the body was stolen ; that it was stolen by the disciples; and that it was stolen when the soldiers slept. If they were asleep, how could they know whether the body was stolen or walked away, or was carried to heaven by the angels ; and if stolen, whether it was by the disciples or by Barabbas, the noted thief? The two parts of the story do not harmonise. If they were asleep, their testimony was utterly worthless. If they were not asleep, and saw the body go away, then they are false witnesses in saying they were asleep. The improbability of this solution is apparent from the fact that the disciples had nothing to gain by having a stolen corpse on hand, with no place to secrete it, and with the certainty of being detected and punished. Besides, there is no record of any search being made for the corpse. If the chief priests could have produced that dead body, the refutation of the claim that He had risen would have been complete. This they were never able to do. Being assured of freedom from danger, the soldiers "took the money, and did as they were taught." Improbable as was this story, the priests were not deceived in their expectation. Perhaps through fear, it was received and circulated. For it is added that "this saying is commonly reported among the Jews until this day."

The question naturally arises, Were those who saw Christ after His resurrection competent witnesses? Were they sufficiently numerous; were they truthful; were they so well acquainted with Him as not to be deceived? That full confidence may be felt in the witnesses of the resurrection, it is important to understand their intelligence, their temperament, and their character. Sufficient facts in the history of those already adduced have been given to establish confidence in them. The same course will be pursued with regard to those still to be introduced. It will appear from the sketch we give that they were competent and trustworthy witnesses, because they had known Him intimately, they were familiar with His person, His countenance, His tones of voice, His ways and habits. So they were competent to decide whether He was the same person whom they had known when alive, whom they had seen crucified, and whose body had been placed in the tomb of Joseph of Arimathæa. These witnesses, of unimpeachable veracity, saw Him, after His resurrection, spake with Him, and had various demonstrations that He was again a living man.

JOURNEY TO EMMAUS.

Towards the evening of the first day of the week two disciples were on their way " to a village called Emmaus, which was from Jerusalem about threescore furlongs [seven miles]. And they talked together of all these things which had happened." " While they communed together and reasoned, Jesus Himself drew near, and went with them." He said, " What manner of communications are these that ye have one to another, as ye walk, and are sad ? " " And they said unto Him, Concerning Jesus of Nazareth . . . and how the chief priests and our rulers delivered Him to be condemned to death, and have crucified Him. But we trusted that it had been He which should have redeemed Israel." "Redeeming" Israel implied civil redemption, and that He should be a king. They then relate the visit of the women and the disciples to the tomb, and that they found not the body, but saw the angels, who said He was alive. Then the Lord so "expounded unto them in all the scriptures the things concerning Himself," that their "hearts burned within them."

"Their eyes were holden that they should not know Him." Possibly this want of recognition was owing to a supernatural influence; or it may have been from an alteration in garb and general appearance. When He was crucified He was stripped, and His garments were divided by the soldiers. His clothes, after His leaving the tomb, were different from what He had formerly worn. Again, it is said "He appeared in another form unto two of them, as they walked, and went into the country." This "another form," as the Greek word clearly intimates, was external form or appearance, in the change of which the unusual garment may have had a share.

Drawing near to the village " He made as though He would have gone further." And, doubtless, He would have gone further had they not invited Him to abide with them : for Christ will not force His continuance upon any who do not desire Him. Their hospitable invitation was accepted, and " He went in to tarry with them." "And it came to pass, as He sat at meat with them, He took bread, and blessed it, and brake, and gave to them. And their eyes were opened, and they knew Him." His manner, His natural tones, His countenance, and possibly the wounds in His hands, as He handed them the bread, flashed conviction upon them that this was the risen Saviour. As they had walked by the way, the dusky twilight was approaching. At the table they were in a lighted room. On the way, they had no perfect view of Him, but when brought to the light they recognised Him. On the way they were despondent and sad, nay, hopeless ; not expecting to see Him again: still, His familiarity with the Scriptures, and His expositions of Moses and all the prophets as bearing upon Jesus of Nazareth, caused their hearts to burn within them, and prepared them for recognising Him when He brake and gave to them the bread. So deeply impressed were they with the fact that He was alive again, that they immediately returned to Jerusalem and found the eleven, "and told what things were done in the way, and how He was known of them in breaking of bread." Mark adds of the disciples, "neither believed they them." This shows their caution. They did not receive the report either of the women or of these men with enthusiasm. They would not commit themselves upon mere hearsay evidence; they must see Him for themselves, and know from tangible testimony that Christ was really alive again.

WITH THE TEN.

This meeting, one of the most important items of proof, occurred on the evening of the first day of the week, all the apostles being present but Thomas. "The doors were shut for fear of the Jews." Christ suddenly "appeared in the midst" of them. As they did not expect Him, when they saw some Being, in human form, enter through the bolted door, whose dress they did not recognise, it is no wonder "they were terrified and affrighted, and supposed they had seen a spirit." The opinion was prevalent in that day that either the spirit of the dead person or his guardian angel appeared, assuming his form and voice. This was not more absurd then than the belief, at a later day, which has possessed true Christians, in witchcraft and other superstitions. This militates no whit against the reality of the resurrection of Christ. The disciples must be judged by the current beliefs of their day. Christ quieted them, saying, "Peace be unto you." He next "upbraided them with their unbelief and hardness of heart, because they believed not them which had seen Him after He was risen." Then, with wonderful condescension and love, He said, "Why are ye troubled? and why do thoughts arise in your hearts?" What thoughts? Alas, of doubt, of apprehension, of fear lest they had misplaced their confidence in Him as the Messiah. He then recalled how He had taught them that "all things must be fulfilled, which were written in the law of Moses, and in the prophets, and in the psalms, concerning" Himself.

Having "opened their understanding, that they might understand the Scriptures," He gave them the most convincing ocular demonstration that He was not a disembodied spirit, but an actual living man, the very same they had seen crucified and buried. "Behold My hands and My feet, that it is I Myself: handle Me, and see; for a spirit hath not flesh and bones, as ye see Me have." "He showed them His hands and His feet." Was not this enough to dissipate all doubt and to settle their minds in firm faith? No: they "believed not for joy, and wondered." This is a strange mental phenomenon, that joy, springing from what we perceive to be true, should prevent belief and only produce wonder. To chase away every vestige of doubt "He said unto them, Have ye here any meat? And they gave Him a piece of a broiled fish, and of an honeycomb. And He took it, and did eat before them." This, so far as the record goes, was the end of all their doubts: they now knew for a certainty that the crucified One was alive again. "Then were the disciples glad, when they saw the Lord."

Such were the peculiar circumstances and momentous interests of this meeting. Christ had personally appeared to them, had instructed them in the Scriptures fulfilled in Him, had submitted His hands and feet to their inspection, had eaten before them, had removed all their doubts and fears, and thus filled their hearts with joyful confidence. He commissioned them, as His witnesses, His apostles, to preach salvation in His name to every creature. Then He breathed upon them, as a symbol of their receiving the Holy Ghost. Now they knew, with perfect assurance, that their Lord was alive again, and that He was the promised Messiah.

Why the disciples did not immediately go to Galilee after receiving the message from their Lord is not stated. It may be that no specific time was mentioned in the message, and that as the feast of the Passover had not yet ended, they were still detained by it in Jerusalem.

WITH THOMAS AND THE TEN.

The second meeting of the apostles took place in the city, one week later, and in the evening. It is simply stated that "Thomas, called Didymus, was not with them when Jesus came," that is, at the first meeting. Why he alone was absent we are not told. It may be traced perhaps to something distinctive in his natural temperament. From the few glimpses of his history we learn that he was affectionate, impulsive, hasty, and at times rash; sometimes he was overcome by a "dark and morbid melancholy." He was a true disciple, and sincerely attached to Christ. When the Lord expressed His determination, on His way to Bethany, to pass through Jerusalem, where accumulating dangers threatened, Thomas said to his fellow-disciples, "Let us also go, that we may die with Him." Though wayward, and at times slow in apprehending the truth, and cautious in admitting statements except on the clearest evidence, still, when convinced, Thomas had the moral courage to carry out his convictions. His caution adds weight to his testimony.

As things were then in a very unsettled state, and as no man could tell what would be the issue, he may have been unwilling to commit himself by attending that first meeting. He knew that the chief priests were then triumphant, and would long continue their authority and control. As the meeting was with closed doors, "for fear of the Jews," he too may have felt the power of that fear. As his mind was not fully made up as to the report of the women, that they had seen and talked with the Lord, and as he could not see any light in the future, he judged it most prudent not to venture out just then, and by any overt act to commit himself to what might prove a delusion.

In this state of mind, not crediting the statement of the women, he did not expect, any more than did the other disciples, to meet Christ there. He knew that Christ was dead and buried. Of these facts, and the guarding of the sepulchre, he had perfect evidence. Some dim remembrance may have flitted before him that the Lord had intimated that He would "rise on the third day." The report of the women was in keeping with this. But they, though **truthful** persons, may have been deceived. No unimpeachable evidence of **His** having **risen** had yet reached him. To all present human appearances and calculation Christianity had no hope. How, then, could he **suppose that** Christ would be present? **Then why** should he go? **Let him** wait, prudently wait, **and** see what would turn up.

Thomas afterwards found that the consequences of his conduct were very painful. He lost the enjoyment and benefit of that meeting. Had he been there, he would have attained **to** the belief of Christ risen. **He** nearly lost his place as an apostle. When the others were commissioned **he was not.** He missed the Master's words, "Receive the Holy Ghost." Christ **came** to a **meeting, and a** disciple who might **have been** there is out of his place. He **is not only** not blessed, but his heart becomes **hardened.** When his fellow-disciples speak **to** him, he is not prepared for their communications. **He** uses unbecoming language, and wounds their feelings. Christ ought to be expected at every meeting of His **people;** surely then when a disciple is absent, without such a reason as Christ would approve, he must expect great loss. What a week of joy was lost by Thomas! All through its course, when the disciples told him, "We have seen the Lord," he persistently replied, "Except I shall see in His hands the print of the nails, and put my finger into the print of the nails, and thrust my hand into His side, I will not believe." Why he thus spake may not certainly be known. Perhaps he felt self-condemned because he had been absent, but was not willing to confess his fault. This made him all the more positive. He justified or excused his unbelief by professedly calling only for reasonable evidence upon a subject so momentous.

Or, it may be that when he, heard all that was done at the first meeting, and ascertained that the ten had been commissioned as apostles, he was angry that he had been left out. True, it was his own fault; but this only vexed him the more. Nothing will touch some men like omitting their names or dispensing with their services. Poor Thomas, having no appointment, swells in importance, and says, "Except I shall see in His hands the print of the nails, and put *my* finger into the print of the nails, and thrust *my* hand into His side, *I* will not believe." Who is this great *I*? It is poor Thomas, whom the Lord could do without. It is Thomas, fretting under his own wrong-doing, and too mean and too proud to confess his wrong; for meanness and pride generally go together. Under the writhings of his wounded pride, he presumptuously tells what *he* will and will not do, as though the cause of Christ depended upon him! Alas, there are too many in every age of the same spirit, slow to believe, and egotistically vain of the very incredulity which withers up their joys.

Thomas was unkind to his brethren. I will not dwell upon the fact that, seemingly, to put the best construction upon it, he deserted them at the very time they most needed his presence and co-operation. They were in great sorrow: mighty powers were triumphing. This, of all others, was the time when Thomas should have been with them, heart to heart, each strengthening and encouraging the other. What a chill it must have cast upon the assembly, what a dagger it must have been in their hearts, when they saw that Thomas was not present! One of their number, they knew, had apostatised and betrayed their Lord. His place was vacated. And where now is Thomas? Has he also gone over to their enemies? It was inconsiderate, at least, whatever his motive, in Thomas to be absent at such a time. But when the disciples met him, his conduct was equally ungenerous and unkind. He paid no regard to their testimony. Yet they were men of integrity, and worthy of his confidence. He had known them to be honest men, incapable of conspiring to deceive him. All ten testify the same thing,—"We have seen the Lord." He would not take their word.

Now all this came from being absent from the meeting. For those who attended it did not distrust one another. It was only the one who was not present who could so cruelly treat his brethren as to distrust their word. Oh, how true it is that a cold heart is an unkind heart! Hear this man. His brethren meet him, and he perhaps inquires, What news have you to-day? Most blessed news, brother Thomas! "We have seen the Lord." He has risen from the dead, as He told us He would. With warmth Thomas exclaims, Poor deluded souls! you are too credulous. Some person has made fools of you. You are too enthusiastic, and ready to believe anything, being carried away with your feelings. And now do you think to impose upon me? I tell you, nay: "Except I shall see in His hands the print of the nails, and put my finger into the print of the nails, and thrust my hand into His side, I will not believe." I must have rational evidence!

Alas! how many thus unkindly judge their brethren! They do not attend the precious meetings where Christ is present according to His promise, and where the Holy Ghost is richly poured out, and consequently their hearts remain cold and worldly. In this frame of mind they judge their brethren, whose hearts have been revived and warmed. Nay, they condemn as irrational the spiritual experiences of their fellow church members. They call them enthusiasts, carried away by mere animal excitement, when they have really been moved by the Holy Ghost. They will not believe them when told of the presence of the Saviour and of the power of the Spirit, and the conversion of sinners. They practically exclude the supernatural from religion, and treat with cold contempt the religious experience of those who meet and commune with the Lord where prayer is appointed to be made. The example of Thomas is widely imitated, though perhaps unconsciously. Theirs is a fearful loss who neglect those meetings where Christ has promised to attend and leave His blessing. " Where two or three are gathered together in My name, there am I in the midst of them."

Thomas both tempted and limited his Lord's power when he prescribed the only way in which he would be convinced. How rash was his determination! How could he know that a risen body must necessarily bear print of the nails and the wound in the side? How could he know that the Saviour would allow him thus to handle Him? And yet, Thomas would not believe unless on these conditions. And what if they had failed?

Why, Thomas would have lost his soul! He would then have been an unbeliever in the resurrection, and consequently of the atonement, and would thus have perished as an apostate. The blessed Saviour saw the peril of Thomas: saw that there was no way of delivering him from his terrible condition but to comply with his unreasonable demand. How unconquerable is the Saviour's love!

"Then came Jesus, the doors being shut, and stood in the midst, and said, Peace be unto you." Then fastening upon Thomas His intensely searching and penetrating, though kind and loving eye, He said, "Thomas, reach hither thy finger, and behold My hands; and reach hither thy hand, and thrust it into My side; and be not faithless, but believing." What a moment of deep thrilling interest, of fear and hope! How condescending, how gracious in our Lord! How tender, yet severe the rebuke! How cut to the heart and thoroughly humbled was Thomas! He has no excuses to offer. His full heart will allow him to utter only the language of affection, submission, and confidence: "MY LORD AND MY GOD!"

This was not a mere exclamation of surprise, but a frank declaration of his belief, Thou art my Lord, and I worship Thee as my God. That he might be confirmed in this humbled, penitent, and believing frame, "Jesus saith unto him, Thomas, because thou hast seen me, thou hast believed; blessed are they that have not seen, and yet have believed." It will be observed that Thomas had drawn back from his irreverent demand when the Lord so graciously complied with it: "Because thou hast *seen* Me:" not "touched" or "handled." The manifestation of Jesus conquers unbelief at once!

We notice with interest that this one rebuke seems to have cured Thomas from staying away from the meetings of the disciples. In subsequent gatherings it is particularly stated that Thomas was there.[1] But as good often comes out of the very waywardness and unbelief of men, the conviction gathers strength that Thomas attained to full confidence in the resurrection only when the evidence was such as to preclude any further hesitancy. Thomas's testimony is the more

[1] See John xxi. 2; Acts i. 13.

valuable because of his stubborn caution. **He doubted, that we might believe.**

THE SEVEN AT TIBERIAS.

Matthew says, " Then the eleven disciples went away into Galilee." This was in obedience to the message which the Lord had sent them by the women. The evangelist John gives a detailed account of this **meeting.** " Jesus showed Himself again to the disciples at the Sea of Tiberias; and on this wise showed He Himself. There were together Simon Peter, and Thomas called Didymus, and Nathanael of Cana in Galilee, and the sons of Zebedee, and two other of His disciples." These men were again on their old "camping ground." They had come to this place to meet their Lord. They had probably waited for Him some days. As He did not appear, they would not loiter about as idlers. The boats, with the nets, were near by on the shore. " Simon Peter saith unto them, I go a fishing. They say unto him, We also go with thee. They went forth, and entered into a ship immediately; and that night they caught nothing." At early dawn "**Jesus** stood on the shore," the boat being distant "two hundred cubits," or three hundred feet. In the misty twilight they "knew not that it was Jesus." He "saith unto them, Children, have ye any meat? They answered Him, No. And He said unto them, Cast the net on the right side of the ship, and ye shall find. They cast therefore, and now they were not able to draw it for the multitude of fishes." The quick ear of John caught the well-known tone of the voice, and his active mind detected the Divine power in the draught of fishes, and he knew it was Jesus. He "saith unto Peter, It is the Lord." Warm-hearted, impetuous Peter "cast himself into the sea," and swam ashore. The others followed in their boat, "dragging the net with fishes." On reaching land "they saw a fire of coals there, and fish laid thereon, and bread." Jesus bade them bring of the "hundred and fifty and three" fishes they had caught, and said, " Come and dine."

A strange fact is now stated. " And none of the disciples durst ask him, Who art thou?" The reason for this conduct is also very strange, "knowing that it was the

Lord." Were they struck dumb with awe and veneration? Or was it that the evidence was so complete that the most credulous durst not, by questioning, desire any further proof? Then Jesus "taketh bread, and giveth them, and fish likewise." It is added, "This is now the third time that Jesus showed Himself to His disciples, after that He was risen from the dead." This must be understood as referring exclusively to His appearing to His *assembled* disciples, viz. on the two evenings at Jerusalem and now at the Lake of Tiberias.

It was at this gathering that Christ had that remarkable and searching interview with Peter personally, which took out of him all his pride and self-sufficiency, and made of him a different man through the remainder of his life. "Jesus saith to Simon Peter, Simon, son of Jonas, lovest thou Me more than these?" The form of the question would stir up much thought in the mind of Peter. Why call me "Simon, *son of Jonas?*" This was my name before He made me His disciple; then He changed it to Simon Peter. Does the Lord mean to disown me by withdrawing the name He gave me? I know that the Scriptures always speak of backsliders in the language appropriate to the unconverted. Surely, I did terribly backslide when I so persistently denied Him. How could I then be discriminated from an enemy? No wonder He withdraws the name He gave me! How significant that question, "Lovest thou Me *more than these?*" What does He mean? When He declared, "All ye shall be offended because of Me this night," did I not say, "Though all men shall be offended because of Thee, yet will I never be offended." And when He said to me that "before the cock crow twice thou shalt deny Me thrice," so foolish and self-confident was I, that I "spake the more vehemently, If I should die with Thee, I will not deny Thee in any wise." Alas! alas! how mean and cowardly I was! I did deny Him thrice, with oaths and curses. I then thought my love greater than that of my fellow disciples. The Lord presses the question, and virtually says, What dost thou now think? They forsook Me; but they did not deny Me. These questions and searchings of heart humbled Peter, and he said,

"Thou knowest that I love thee." The Lord said to him "the second time, Simon, son of Jonas, lovest thou Me?" Not more than others; but dost thou love Me at all? This searched deeper. Peter more decidedly says, "Yea, Lord, Thou knowest that I love Thee." Christ, to uproot his self sufficient and self-confident spirit, "saith to him the third time, Simon, son of Jonas, lovest thou Me?" Peter, from these repetitions, and the terrible words "son of Jonas," feared that the Lord still doubted the sincerity of his love, and was grieved. The thrice-repeated question might well grieve him. It reminded him of his thrice-repeated denial of Christ. Heartbroken and penitent, he appeals to His omniscience: "Lord, Thou knowest all things; Thou knowest that I love Thee." Then Peter was fully restored. His apostleship was given back to him in the charge, repeated, like the denial, like the question, "Feed My sheep—Feed My lambs."

The forgiving Lord had met with Peter *alone*, on His resurrection-day. Of that interview no record but the simple fact [1]

[1] See Luke xxiv. 34; 1 Cor. xv. 5.

remains. Yet who can doubt that the words of love then spoken in private prepared the way for this public declaration of love and confidence renewed?

THE FIVE HUNDRED.

Matthew tells us that the disciples went to Galilee, "into a mountain where Jesus had appointed them." From Paul we learn that on this occasion "He was seen of about five hundred brethren at once." Matthew says, "And when they saw Him, they worshipped Him: but some doubted." This doubting, certainly, was not true of any of the eleven apostles, after all the evidence they had had furnished them in Jerusalem and other places. They had already been commissioned as apostles, and commanded to meet Him personally at this time and place. The doubters were among the numerous disciples of Galilee gathered together on this occasion. The statement, by Matthew, that "some doubted" is evidence of the frankness and truthfulness of his narrative.

The Lord had directed that His disciples in Galilee should assemble upon this specified mountain. Whether it was Tabor or the Mountain of Beatitudes is not known. This was the solemn closing of His ministry in Galilee, where He had spent most of His life; where most of His miracles had been wrought, where He had so frequently taught, and where His disciples were the most numerous. It was to this vast concourse of disciples that He said, "All power is given unto Me in heaven and earth. Go ye therefore, and teach [disciple] all nations, baptizing them in the name of the Father, and of the Son, and of the Holy Ghost: teaching them to observe all things whatsoever I have commanded you : and, lo, I am with you alway, even unto the end of the world. Amen." This command to do His work among the "nations," and this gracious assurance of His presence, "even to the end of the world," were given not alone to the eleven apostles, but to the assembled multitude of disciples. This teaches that it is not the exclusive duty of those professionally devoted to the ministry to disciple men to Christ, but the duty and privilege of every true disciple to labour to make disciples of others. How this command was understood by the early disciples is thus stated: "Therefore they that were scattered abroad went everywhere preaching the word."

OTHER TESTIMONIES.

Not to break the chain of evidence, we here present, out of the order of time, certain facts of a peculiar character, which bear with intense force upon the question of the resurrection of Christ. These facts had their existence after the ascension, but they bring the parties most interested face to face. On the day of Pentecost, "Peter, standing up with the eleven, lifted up his voice, and said unto them, Ye men of Judæa, and all ye that dwell at Jerusalem, be this known unto you, and hearken to my words . . . Jesus of Nazareth, a man approved of God among you by miracles and wonders and signs, which God did by Him in the midst of you, as ye yourselves also know: Him, being delivered by the determinate counsel and foreknowledge of God, ye have taken, and by wicked hands have crucified and slain: whom God hath raised up, having loosed the pains of death: because it was not possible that He should be holden of it." This is a bold and unflinching statement of the death and resurrection of Christ. His crucifixion by the hands of the lawless [Gentiles] is charged upon the Jews, and His resurrection by Divine power is asserted. To the facts of the death and the resurrection there was no denial by those present, who knew the facts.

When Peter, at the Beautiful Gate of the Temple, healed the man "lame from his mother's womb," and the people were "greatly wondering," he said, "Ye men of Israel, why marvel ye at this? or why look ye so earnestly on us, as though by our own power or holiness we had made this man to walk? The God of Abraham, and of Isaac, and of Jacob, the God of our fathers, hath glorified His Son Jesus; whom ye delivered up, and denied Him in the presence of Pilate, when he was determined to let Him go. But ye denied the Holy One and the Just, and desired a murderer to be granted unto you; and killed the Prince of life, whom God hath raised from the dead; whereof we are witnesses." This statement not only names the crucifixion and resurrection as real, but appeals to certain facts too well known to be denied, and boldly asserts that this Jesus is the "Son of God," and therefore Divine. It was for claiming to be the Son of God that Christ was pronounced a blasphemer, and therefore condemned to death. Yet Peter reaffirms this claim, and authenticates it by appealing to the resurrection, by which God hath glorified His Son.

When the apostles were brought before the "rulers, and elders, and scribes, and Annas the high priest, and Caiaphas," and others, and asked, "By what power, or by what name, have ye done this?" Peter said, "Ye rulers of the people, and elders of Israel, . . . be it known unto you all, and to all the people of Israel, that by the name of Jesus Christ of Nazareth, whom ye crucified, whom God raised from the dead, even by Him doth this man stand here before you whole." Here the facts of the death and resurrection are asserted, and are not denied by the rulers, elders, scribes, and chief priests, even when the crucifixion is directly charged upon them. These men in authority, the responsible agents, who could not deny either the facts or their agency, " were grieved " that these men taught the people, and preached, through Jesus, " the resurrection from the dead." They " commanded them not to speak at all, nor teach in the name of Jesus." The apostles went on with their preaching " Jesus and the resurrection," and " many signs and wonders were wrought [by them] among the people." This demonstration greatly excited the indignation of the high priest, and all that were with him, and "they laid their hands on the apostles, and put them in the common prison." On the morrow, when the high priest had convened " all the senate of the children of Israel," and found that the apostles were not in the prison, but in the Temple, preaching to the people " Jesus and the resurrection," " they doubted of them whereunto this would grow." When brought before the council, the high priest said, " Did not we straitly command you that ye should not teach in this name ? and, behold, ye have filled Jerusalem with your doctrine, and intend to bring this man's blood upon us." Here there is no denial either of the death or the resurrection, but fear that the people should regard the crucifixion of Christ as a wilful murder, and the chief priests and council as the murderers. But Peter and the other apostles were not intimidated; they answered, "We ought to obey God rather than men." They again boldly charge the rulers with His death, and fearlessly proclaim the resurrection and glorification of Christ. "The God of our fathers raised up Jesus, whom ye slew and hanged on a tree. Him hath God exalted with His right hand to be a Prince and a Saviour, for to give repentance to Israel, and forgiveness of sins. And we are His witnesses of these things; and so is also the Holy Ghost, whom God hath given to them that obey Him." This unconquerable determination of these despised men to charge the rulers as the murderers of an innocent man they could stand no longer. When they heard this last testimony, they were filled, not with penitence, but with vengeance; "they were cut to the heart," and as they could make no defence, "they took counsel to slay them." In all these transactions, neither the crucifixion nor the resurrection of Christ is denied by the high priest and the rulers. These facts are, through threatenings and intimidations and imprisonment, stedfastly declared and unflinchingly proclaimed. Wherever the apostles went they preached "Jesus and the resurrection."[1]

The apostle Paul in his first letter to the Corinthians thus sums up the evidence for the resurrection : "For I delivered unto you first of all that which I also received, how that Christ died for our sins according to the Scriptures ; and that He was buried, and that He rose again the third day according to the Scriptures : and that He was seen of Cephas, then of the twelve : after that, He was seen of above five hundred brethren at once ; of whom the greater part remain unto this present, but some are fallen asleep. After that, He was seen of James ; then of all the apostles. And last of all He was seen of me also, as of one born out of due time." This is the testimony of the man who thought he "ought to do many things contrary to the name of Jesus of Nazareth," and who persecuted unto

[1] See Acts xiii. 29-37 ; xvii. 18.

the death, binding and delivering into prisons both men and women, and at whose feet, as the approving witness, they laid the clothes of the martyr Stephen. This is the man who says, "And last of all He was seen of me." Had Paul never seen Christ before He was crucified? What if he had? That was not enough. To be an apostle, and a sufficient witness for Christ, it was necessary that he should have seen Him bodily after his resurrection. "One must be ordained to be a witness of His resurrection." Accordingly, when Saul of Tarsus was on his persecuting mission to Damascus, "yet breathing out threatenings and slaughter against the disciples of the Lord," "suddenly there shined round about him a light from heaven, and he fell to the earth, and heard a voice, saying unto him, Saul, Saul, why persecutest thou Me? And he said, Who art Thou, Lord?" And the Lord said, "I am Jesus, whom thou persecutest. And he, trembling and astonished, said, Lord, what wilt Thou have me to do?" Then it was that this "last of all the witnesses" saw Jesus after His resurrection. This appearance was special. To qualify him to be an apostle, the Lord showed Himself to Him bodily, with all the evidences of identity, and said, "I have appeared unto thee for this purpose, to make thee a minister and a witness both of these things which thou hast seen, and of those things in the which I will appear unto thee." "For thou shalt be a witness unto all men of what thou hast seen and heard." His seeing the risen Lord in His body as crucified was the essential prerequisite to his being an apostle—"a chosen vessel to bear the name of Christ before the Gentiles, and kings, and children of Israel."

What if the women, with Joseph of Arimathæa and Nicodemus and the disciples, had, on the third day, come to the sepulchre and found the stone undisturbed? What if, on entering the tomb, they had found the body there cold in death? What if they had completed the burial preparations and rolled back the stone? What if, after weeks, they had again entered the tomb, and found the body still there, with certain evidences of progressing dissolution, how changed and hopeless the destinies of the whole world!

The death on the cross would not have been an atonement, but the execution of a deluded enthusiast, if not of a criminal impostor. The resurrection is the central fact of Christianity. "If Christ be not raised, your faith is vain; ye are yet in your sins."[1] "Declared to be the Son of God with power, according to the Spirit of holiness, by the resurrection from the dead."[2] When He arose the atonement offered was accepted, and salvation made free.

[1] 1 Cor. xv. 17.   [2] Rom. i. 4.

XII.

THE ASCENSION.

CHAPTER XII.

THE ASCENSION.

IN direct personal evidence of His resurrection we last saw our Lord on one of the mountains of Galilee, surrounded by " above five hundred brethren." We next hear of Him at Jerusalem, with "the apostles whom He had chosen : to whom also He showed Himself alive after His passion by many infallible proofs, being seen of them forty days, and speaking of the things pertaining to the kingdom of God." What these teachings were during those eventful forty days, we are not specifically told. Doubtless they included the fuller opening up to them of the Scriptures concerning Himself, as He did to the two disciples on their way to Emmaus; with more distinct revelations of the extent and power of His atonement made by His death on the cross; and, assuredly, the renewed promise of the Holy Spirit, the Comforter, now that He was soon to leave them.

In keeping with this, He "commanded them that they should not depart from Jerusalem, but wait for the promise of the Father, which ye have heard of Me." "Ye shall be baptized with the Holy Ghost not many days hence." "Behold, I send the promise of My Father upon you: but tarry ye in the city of Jerusalem until ye be endued with power from on high." "Ye shall receive power, after that the Holy Ghost is come upon you: and ye shall be witnesses unto Me both in Jerusalem, and in all Judæa, and in Samaria, and unto the uttermost part of the earth." As the Lord spake of the "things pertaining to the kingdom of God," the disciples, whose minds were not yet purged from the idea of a temporal monarchy, asked Him. "Lord, wilt Thou at this time restore again the kingdom to Israel?" He rebuked them, saying, "It is not for you to know the times or the seasons, which the Father hath put in His own power." It is enough for you to know that "all power is given unto Me in heaven and in earth," and that I send you to "preach the gospel to every creature," "beginning at Jerusalem."

These teachings were delivered as they passed over the brook Cedron and wound their way up the Mount of Olives. "And He led them out as far as to Bethany, and He lifted up His hands, and blessed them. And it came to pass, while He blessed them, He was parted from them, and carried up into heaven." "He was taken up; and a cloud received Him out of their sight. And while they looked stedfastly toward heaven as He went up, behold, two men stood by them in white apparel; which also said, Ye men of Galilee, why stand ye gazing up into heaven? this same Jesus, which is taken up from you into heaven, shall so come in like manner as ye have seen Him go into heaven." "And they worshipped Him, and returned to Jerusalem with great joy: and were continually in the temple, praising and blessing God." Such is the simple statement of this most august event. It stands grand and glorious,—

> "Like the cerulean arch we see,
> Majestic in its own simplicity."

His last earthly act was a benediction. "While He blessed them, He was parted from them,"—"was taken up," "was received up into heaven." No external force was manifest. In apparent opposition to the law of gravitation, His body, by His own will, ascended, "and a cloud received Him out of their sight." "A bright cloud," the symbol of the Divine presence, had "overshadowed" the scene when the Lord was transfigured. That transfiguration, when "His face did shine as the sun, and His raiment was white as the light," illustrates what the glorified bodies of the saints shall be when they shall be like Him "who shall change our vile body, that it may be fashioned like unto His glorious body." As "flesh and blood cannot inherit the kingdom of God," so "there is a natural body, and there is a spiritual body." It is reasonable to believe that as our Lord ascended from Olivet, His body was changed from that which was fleshly and mortal to that which was spiritual and immortal.

"He was received up into heaven, and sat on the right hand of God." So testify the Scriptures: "Who is gone into heaven, and is on the right hand of God; angels and authorities and powers being made subject unto Him." "Who being the brightness of His glory, and the express image of His person, and upholding all things by the word of His power, when He had by Himself purged our sins, sat down on the right hand of the Majesty on high." "Which He wrought in Christ, when He raised Him from the dead, and set Him at His own right hand in the heavenly places."

"They looked stedfastly toward heaven as He went up," until "a cloud received Him out of their sight." How long their loving hearts would have kept them gazing and wondering and filled with awe cannot be surmised. The Lord cuts short this up-gazing by sending two messengers with a revelation to them, "Behold, two men stood by them in white apparel; which also said,

Ye men of Galilee, why stand ye gazing up into heaven? This same Jesus, which is taken up from you into heaven, shall so come in like manner as ye have seen Him go into heaven." When and where this shall have its fulfilment the Lord has not revealed. The prophet Daniel says, "I saw in the night visions, and, behold, one like the Son of man came with the clouds of heaven." And the apostle says, "The Lord Himself shall descend from heaven with a shout, with the voice of the archangel." "The Lord Jesus shall be revealed from heaven with His mighty angels." "And unto them that look for Him shall He appear the second time without sin unto salvation."[1] Were these two messengers the same whom the women saw at the sepulchre?—"two men stood by them in shining garments, and said unto them, Why seek ye the living among the dead?" Were they the "two men, Moses and Elijah, who appeared in glory," and talked with Christ, and "spake of His decease which He should accomplish at Jerusalem?" There was a manifest pro-

[1] Dan. vii. 13; 1 Thess. iv. 16; 2 Thess. i. 7; Heb. ix. 28.

priety that Moses the lawgiver, and Elijah the great prophet, should meet their Lord in their glorified bodies on the mount, and there speak of the atonement about to be made, on which they, with prospective faith, relied for salvation. Equally appropriate was it, that they should watch in His tomb and announce His resurrection, which was the evidence of the completed atonement; and not less so that they should be present at the ascension, and reveal the fact that the Lord should return again from heaven.

What we know with certainty is, that the disciples "worshipped Him." This they could not have done unless confident that He was the Divine Messiah, the Son of God. That they thus believed they testified by their lives of devotion to Christ and suffering for Him. With the unclouded conviction that He was the Messiah, to whom "all power was given in heaven and in earth," they "returned to Jerusalem with great joy: and were continually in the temple, praising and blessing God."

The evangelist John, in closing his narrative, says, "And many other signs truly did Jesus in the presence of His disciples, which are not written in this book: but these are written, that ye might believe that Jesus is the Christ, the Son of God; and that believing ye might have life through His name."

"*Jesus*," who saves His people from their sins; "*Christ*," the anointed One, the great High Priest, the Messiah,[1] "*the Son of God*," the Divine Redeemer, through whom, by faith in His name, every man may secure eternal life. And this offer not for a day, a year, a century, but for all time. "Jesus Christ, the same yesterday, to-day, and for ever." Blessed Jesus, how imperishable and unchangeable is Thy love!

[1] John i. 41; iv. 25.

XIII.

THE GIFT OF THE HOLY SPIRIT.

CHAPTER XIII.

THE GIFT OF THE HOLY SPIRIT.

THE apostles abode in Jerusalem. They continued in prayer, waiting for the promised "baptism of the Holy Ghost," by which they were endowed with power to "preach repentance and remission of sins in His name, among all nations, beginning at Jerusalem." On the day of Pentecost the promise of the Spirit was fulfilled, and the dispensation of the Spirit was inaugurated. The apostles were "filled with the Holy Ghost, and began to speak with other tongues, as the Spirit gave them utterance." The three thousand then and there in a few hours converted, were not the limit, but only the sample of the power. It was given for the encouragement of all the ages. It was but the handful of first-fruits which betokened the abundant harvest.

To cheer the sorrowing disciples, the Lord had said, "It is expedient for you that I go away: for if I go not away, the Comforter will not come unto you; but if I depart, I will send Him unto you. And when He is come, He will reprove the world of sin, and of righteousness, and of judgment."[1] "I will pray the Father, and He shall give you another Comforter, that He may abide with you for ever; even the Spirit of truth." "The Comforter, which is the Holy Ghost, whom the Father will send in My name, He shall teach you all things." "But when the Comforter is come, whom I will send unto you from the Father, even the Spirit of truth, which proceedeth from the Father, He shall testify of Me."[2] "Behold, I send the promise of My Father upon you."[3] Thus ran the promise, "I will pour My Spirit upon thy seed, and My blessing upon thine offspring."[4] "I will pour out my Spirit

---

[1] John xvi. 7, 8.   [2] John xiv. 16; xiv. 26; xv. 26.
[3] Luke xxiv. 49.   [4] Isa. xliv. 3.

upon all flesh."[1] The promise that the kingdom of the Messiah should be universal also designated the Holy Spirit as the efficient power. "I will pour out My Spirit unto you;" "Not by might, nor by power, but by My Spirit, saith the Lord of hosts." "Behold My Servant, whom I have chosen; My Beloved, in whom My soul is well pleased: I will put My Spirit upon Him, and He shall show judgment to the Gentiles."[2] Answering to these assurances of the elder times, comes the response of the new dispensation: "The Spirit of the Lord is upon Me, because He hath anointed Me to preach the gospel to the poor; He hath sent Me to heal the broken-hearted, to preach deliverance to the captives, and recovering of sight to the blind, to set at liberty them that are bruised, to preach the acceptable year of the Lord. . . . And He began to say unto them, This day is this scripture fulfilled in your ears."[3]

The Holy Spirit, the third Person of the adorable Trinity, as promised, was given by Christ as the efficient agent for carrying out to triumphant completion the grand

[1] Joel ii. 28.   [2] Matt. xii. 18.   [3] Luke iv. 18, 19, 21.

remedial scheme. The Holy Spirit is Christ's gift to the world. Until the atonement was made, in the person and by the death of Jesus the Son of God, the dispensation of the Spirit could not be inaugurated. Upon the ascension of Christ, the omnipotent, omniscient, and omnipresent Spirit commenced His mission. His immediate and extraordinary work was to endue the apostles with power from on high,—to qualify them by influences and miraculous forces to fulfil their commission to preach the Gospel, to complete the volume of inspiration, and to establish Christianity upon an ever-enduring and immovable foundation.

In securing the salvation of men, He neither creates new faculties nor originates moral responsibility, nor reveals new truth, but makes the truth vital. "The word of God . . . is a discerner of the thoughts and intents of the heart."[1] Animated by the same love with the Father and the Son, He prosecutes His work with intense interest and affection. He is ever waiting to be gracious. It was at Jerusalem, the most

[1] Heb. iv. 12.

guilty and hopeless of cities, that the first effusion of the Spirit took place. There is no possibility of exhausting the power of the omnipotent Spirit; there is no possibility of limiting the searching force of the omniscient Spirit; there is no possibility of shutting out the presence of the omnipresent Spirit. With such appliances the apostles went forth, confident that wherever the providence of God should carry them, there they would find the Spirit present and ready to bless His own Word and to work with them, if they were ready to work for Christ. They, being full of the Holy Ghost, "so spake that a great multitude both of the Jews and of the Greeks believed." Barnabas was "a good man, and full of the Holy Ghost and of faith; and much people was added to the Lord." It is not all kinds of speaking the truth that win the heart; but so speaking that the truth, as revealed, shall stand out quick and powerful, a discerner of the thoughts and intents of the heart and a reprover of sin. Christ, knowing the power of the truth, as the sword of the Spirit, cheered His apostles with the assurance that "in that generation," before the destruction of Jerusalem was accomplished, "the gospel of the kingdom shall be preached in all the world, for a witness unto all nations." The Acts of the Apostles presents a series of instructive and encouraging illustrations of the agency of the Spirit. It was, and remains through all time, the work of Christ Himself. The record of His earthly life sets forth "the things which Jesus *began* both to do and teach."[1] The subsequent history of the church disclosed His *continued* workings by His Spirit.

For the work of the Holy Spirit is a distinctive part of the mission of Christ. He promised to send the Spirit to " reprove [convict] the world of sin." He said He would pray the Father to give "the Spirit of truth to abide for ever:" Who "would teach all things." He said that the Holy Spirit would testify of Him; that He would "guide into all truth: for He shall not speak of Himself; but whatsoever He shall hear, that shall He speak: and He will show you things to come. He shall glorify Me : for He shall receive of Mine, and shall show it unto you."[2]

[1] Acts i. 1. [2] John xvi. 13, 14.

The blessed, omnipotent, and omnipresent Spirit is the executive agent to carry out the work of salvation, now that Christ has ascended to His mediatorial throne in the heavens. The Holy Spirit is included in the "all power given unto Me in heaven and in earth;" "Head over all things to the church;" "I am with you alway unto the end of the world." Harmoniously acting, the Holy Spirit is intensely set, with one purpose, on glorifying the work of Christ in dying for the salvation of men. The doctrines of the cross, which the Holy Ghost in all ages blesses, cluster around Jesus Christ. He is the central figure and the unfailing power. His incarnation, His death, His resurrection, and His ascension are the cardinal, vitalising facts by which the Divine Spirit has reanimated, and will continue to reanimate, a perishing world, changing it from sin to holiness. "Casting down imaginations, and every high thing that exalteth itself against the knowledge of God, and bringing into captivity every thought to the obedience of Christ."[1]

[1] 2 Cor. x. 5.

In the fifteenth chapter of the first Epistle to the Corinthians the Apostle Paul gives an extended illustration of the manner in which, by the power of the Holy Spirit, he commended the truth to the souls of men:

"I declare unto you the gospel which I preached unto you, which also ye have received, and wherein ye stand; by which also ye are saved, if ye keep in memory what I preached unto you. . . . For I delivered unto you first of all that which I also received, how that Christ died for our sins according to the Scriptures; and that He was buried, and that He rose again the third day according to the Scriptures." He dwells not mainly upon the dead, but the living Christ. He carefully spreads out the evidences of the resurrection, and shows how fundamental that fact is to Christianity. "If there be no resurrection of the dead, then is Christ not risen: and if Christ be not risen, then is our preaching vain, and your faith is also vain. Ye are yet in your sins. Then they also which are fallen asleep in Christ are perished." "But now is Christ risen from the dead, and become the first-fruits of them that slept." He cheers them with the assurance that the risen Christ has ascended to heaven, is seated upon the mediatorial throne ; has all power, and an ever-widening kingdom ; that " He must reign until He hath put all enemies under His feet." He comforts them with the certainty of their own resurrection, with spiritual bodies admirably adapted to their then spiritual and eternal condition. " So when this corruptible shall have put on incorruption, and this mortal shall have put on immortality, then shall be brought to pass the saying that is written, Death is swallowed up in victory." Under the cheering power of these sublime truths, he bursts forth in strains of exulting triumph, "O death, where is thy sting? O grave, where is thy victory? . . . Thanks be to God, which giveth us the victory through our Lord Jesus Christ." He closes his discourse by urging the necessary and imperative practical consequence of the full belief in " Jesus and the resurrection." "Therefore, my beloved brethren, be ye stedfast, unmovable, always abounding in the work of the Lord, forasmuch as ye know that your labour is not in vain in the Lord." "Jesus and the resurrection" was an element of comfort as well as of power. The death of Christ, the atoning sacrifice, was the only reliance of the first teachers of the Gospel for the pardon of sin, the perfect cleansing from its pollution, and the triumph over it. The resurrection and kingly authority of Christ were the source of their confidence and their courage. This made them "stedfast and unmovable" when opposition, with malignant rage, compassed them about; made them cheerful and hopeful, and abounding in their work, until it spread Christianity, through persecutions the most stubbornly cruel and relentlessly persevering, over the Roman Empire. "Whom we preach, warning every man, and teaching every man in all wisdom; that we may present every man perfect in Christ Jesus : whereunto I also labour, striving according to His working, which worketh in me mightily." [1]

With the conviction, as intense and real as in their own existence, that all men are sinners; that all are condemned by God's

[1] Col. i. 28, 29.

righteous law; that there is no possible hope for the salvation of any one except through the atoning blood of Jesus Christ, and with hearts burning for souls, they went forth, and preached "Jesus and the resurrection." With unwavering confidence in the atonement and in the promised presence of Christ and the Holy Ghost, and knowing, from personal experience, the power of the Gospel to save, they spake to every man with assurance that Christ died, and rose, and reigns for him. Thus, with the double power of hope—hope in the preacher and hope for the guilty—the response was quick, and vast multitudes were added to the Lord.

These truths being fundamental, they must always be the power of God unto salvation. "Blessed be the God and Father of our Lord Jesus Christ, which according to His abundant mercy hath begotten us again unto a lively hope by the resurrection of Jesus Christ from the dead."[1]

"Jesus and the resurrection" are not simply historical facts to be received or rejected. They are life-principles, and essen-

[1] 1 Peter i. 3.

tial to spiritual life. Christ, "the firstfruits of them that slept," makes certain the resurrection of all men. This forces the moral government of God upon the attention, it carries the man beyond the grave, where the awards will be according to the deeds done in the body. This throws deep solemnity upon the life that now is, and makes Christ crucified a most welcome truth, because "He died for our sins." The risen Saviour is the only "hope of glory." "Begotten again unto a lively hope by the resurrection of Jesus Christ from the dead."[1] "For whether we we live, we live unto the Lord; and whether we die, we die unto the Lord: whether we live therefore, or die, we are the Lord's. For to this end Christ both died, and rose, and revived."[2] "I am the resurrection, and the life: he that believeth in Me, though he were dead, yet shall he live: and whosoever liveth and believeth in Me shall never die."[3]

[1] 1 Peter i. 3.   [2] Rom. xiv. 8, 9.   [3] John xi. 25, 26.

XIV.

THE MEDIATORIAL KING.

CHAPTER XIV.

THE MEDIATORIAL KING.

WHEREFORE did the Lord ascend on high? Prophecy answers: "I have set My King upon My holy hill of Zion." "The heathen shall be His inheritance, and the uttermost parts of the earth His possession." "He shall have dominion from sea to sea, and from the river unto the ends of the earth." "His name shall endure for ever, and men shall be blessed in Him: all nations shall call Him blessed." "Let the whole earth be filled with His glory." Such is the prophetic delineation of the universal happy empire of the Mediatorial King. The same love which brought the Lord from heaven to the cross controls His heart whilst sitting upon the mediatorial throne. That He may perfectly and triumphantly carry out the rich and wide-reaching purposes of His atonement, "God hath made that same Jesus both Lord and Christ." "Him hath God exalted to be a Prince and a Saviour, for to give repentance to Israel, and forgiveness of sins."[1] "Wherefore God also hath highly exalted Him, and given Him a name which is above every name: that at the name of Jesus every knee should bow, of things in heaven, and things in earth, and things under the earth; and that every tongue should confess that Jesus Christ is Lord, to the glory of God the Father."[2] "For to this end Christ both died, and rose, and revived, that He might be Lord both of the dead and living."[3]

Prophecy in the distant past foretold the purpose of the mediatorial reign. "Thou hast ascended on high, Thou hast led captivity captive: Thou hast received gifts for men; yea, for the rebellious also, that the Lord God might dwell among them." The answering voice comes, "He ascended up on high, He led captivity captive, and He gave gifts unto men. . . . He gave some,

[1] Acts v. 31.   [2] Phil. ii. 9-11.   [3] Rom. xiv. 9.

apostles; and some, prophets; and some, evangelists; and some, pastors and teachers; for the perfecting of the saints, for the work of the ministry, for the edifying of the body of Christ: till we all come in the unity of the faith, and of the knowledge of the Son of God, unto a perfect man, unto the measure of the stature of the fulness of Christ." [1]

The promised Messiah spake by His prophet: "Look unto Me, and be ye saved, all the ends of the earth: for I am God, and there is none else." "I, even I, am the Lord; and beside Me there is no Saviour." "All the ends of the world shall remember and turn unto the Lord: and all the kindreds of the nations shall worship before Thee."[2] The Messiah answered the prediction,—"As Moses lifted up the serpent in the wilderness, even so must the Son of man be lifted up." "And I, if I be lifted up from the earth, will draw all men unto Me." "Who will have all men to be saved, and come to the knowledge of the truth. For there is one God, and one Mediator between God and men, the man

---

[1] Psa. lxviii. 18; Eph. iv. 8–13.
[2] Isa. xlv. 22; Isa. xliii. 11; Psa. xxii. 27.

Christ Jesus; who gave Himself a ransom for all." "Neither is there salvation in any other: for there is none other name under heaven given among men whereby we must be saved." "The blood of Jesus Christ His Son cleanseth us from all sin."

To carry out the benevolence of the redemptive scheme in all its bearings to the utmost completion, "Jesus, who was made a little lower than the angels for the suffering of death, is crowned with glory," is gone into heaven, and is on the right hand of God; angels, authorities, and powers being made subject unto Him. "For by Him were all things created, that are in heaven, and that are in earth, visible and invisible, whether they be thrones, or dominions, or principalities, or powers: all things were created by Him and for Him." When God "raised Him from the dead," He "set Him at His own right hand in the heavenly places, far above all principality, and power, and might, and dominion, and every name that is named, not only in this world, but also in that which is to come: and hath put all things under His feet, and gave Him to be head over all things to the church, which is His body, the fulness of Him that filleth all in all." "For He must reign, till He hath put all enemies under His feet."

This world, be it remembered, grand as it may seem to us, is hardly a speck in the vast, and to us limitless, material universe. And all the inhabitants, from the beginning to the end, are scarcely an item in the inventory of the countless myriads of intelligent and accountable beings whom God has created. Yet every intelligent being in the universe has a personal and eternal interest in the manifestations of Divine justice and mercy which are here being displayed. The redemptive scheme, by which the guilty are pardoned, the rebellious made loyal, and the polluted purified, is the wonder of heaven. "The angels desire to look into" it. God has revealed the ulterior purposes of the atonement as affecting personally all the pure spirits around His throne. "For it pleased the Father that in Him should all fulness dwell; and, having made peace through the blood of His cross, by Him to reconcile all things unto Himself; by Him,

I say, whether they be things in earth, or things in heaven."[1] "That **He** might gather together in one all things in Christ, both which are in heaven, and which are on earth." "God, who created all things by Jesus Christ, to the intent that now unto the principalities and powers in heavenly places might be known by the church the manifold wisdom of God, according to the eternal purpose which He purposed in Christ Jesus our Lord."[2]

The purpose was eternal: "The Lamb slain from the foundation of the world."[3] By means of the church gathered out of this sinful world, and purged from sin by the blood of Christ, God purposed to make known "His manifold," multifarious, greatly diversified "wisdom" to the principalities and powers in heavenly places. Why make this manifestation? Certainly not for His own gratification, but for their instruction, that they may perfectly understand the true nature of sin, and that their confidence in the rectitude and benevolence of His government might be confirmed with unwavering

[1] Col. i. 19, 20.   [2] Ephes. iii. 9-11.   [3] Rev. xiii. 8.

trust. For here, in this world, as nowhere else, is the true and unalterable nature of sin demonstrated. And here, as nowhere else, is seen that wonder of all wonders, how God can be just, and the Justifier of the ungodly, through the atonement of His Son.

When the angels rebelled, the holy ones saw the meanness, the baseness, and evil of sin. When they were immediately cast out of heaven, the loyal ones saw the deep abhorrence of sin by God. But they could not then know its virulent and relentless malignity. They could not then know what might be the effect of forbearance on the part of God. Who could then tell that the rebellious would not repent if a solitary ray of hope had lighted up their intense darkness and despair? All these and many other things are settled, and settled for ever, by the demonstrations made upon this earth. God has shown the holy ones that He was not cruel when He hurled the devil and his angels into their prison. He means to establish for ever the true nature of sin, by demonstrating, through ages of its diversified treatment, that it takes advantage of the patience, the forbearance, the love, the mercy of God, to go on to deeper depths of malignity and hatred. All this lies open to the view of the heavenly principalities and powers. They can have no misgivings as to the malignant nature of sin, nor as to the degraded and viciously selfish character it always involves, and of the inevitable misery it produces. They must see and understand, and with adoring wonder acknowledge, the manifold wisdom and benevolence of God in His treatment and final disposition of the incorrigibly wicked.

When the grand consummation shall come, and the redeemed from all time are gathered to the realms of the blessed, then it will be found that "where sin abounded, grace did much more abound." Counting all who have died in infancy, whose salvation, as I judge, is secured by the atonement and the Holy Spirit, and including the converts through the long ages of the millennium, when the whole world will be densely populated, I am confident it will be found that the overwhelming mass of human souls will have been saved from the penalty and power of sin by faith in "the blood of the Lamb." The pledge of reward to Christ was, "He shall see of the travail of His soul, and shall be satisfied;"[1] and the record of history is, that He "for the joy that was set before Him endured the cross, despising the shame."[2] "For this purpose the Son of God was manifested, that He might destroy the works of the devil."[3] If, as some would estimate from the present and past history of this world, it should appear that only a small minority are saved, there would be a perpetual jubilee in hell, that Satan had thwarted the Son of God and gained the victory. If it should be found that Christ had secured the salvation of only one-half the human family, Satan would call it a drawn game, and rejoice over his spoils. In either of these cases could the benevolent heart of the Redeemer be "satisfied?" Could it then be said that He had fulfilled His mission to "destroy the works of the devil?" But when it shall come out, clear, distinct, and unquestionable, that the number of the persistently impenitent and incorrigibly

---

[1] Isa. liii. 11.   [2] Heb. xii. 2.   [3] 1 John iii. 8.

wicked, though great, is so comparatively small as only to illustrate the malignant character of sin and the necessity of punishment;—when the great multitude, which no man can number, of all nations, and kindreds, and people, and tongues, shall stand before the throne, and before the Lamb, clothed with white robes, and palms in their hands, crying with a loud voice, Salvation to our God, which sitteth upon the throne, and unto the Lamb; "Salvation, and glory, and honour, and power, unto the Lord our God: for true and righteous are His judgments;"—when the voice of many angels round about the throne, and the living creatures and the elders, the number of them being ten thousand times ten thousand, and thousands of thousands, cry with a loud voice, as they shout the victory, "Worthy is the Lamb that was slain to receive power, and riches, and wisdom, and strength, and honour, and glory, and blessing;" "Blessing, and glory, and wisdom, and thanksgiving, and honour, and power, and might, be unto our God for ever and ever;"—when the redeemed swell again the grateful song, "For Thou wast slain, and hast redeemed us to God by Thy blood out of every kindred, and tongue, and people, and nation;"—and when the triumphal chorus of "every creature which is in heaven, and on the earth, and under the earth, and such as are in the sea, and all that are in them," cry, "Blessing, and honour, and glory, and power, be unto Him that sitteth upon the throne, and unto the Lamb for ever and ever:"—then will the Redeemer say, I AM SATISFIED. I have put all enemies under My feet. I have destroyed the works of the devil. I have utterly and for ever crushed out his kingdom. I have shut him and his followers in their own appropriate place, the prison-house of despair. I have gathered out of that world, ruined by sin, a multitude so vast that no man can number them. I have confirmed in holiness all the principalities and powers in the heavenly places, so that in all the ages there shall never again be a falling away. I have conquered death, the fruit of sin, and abolished it, and there shall be no more dying. I have restored peace and harmony in all the holy empire of God, so that through all eternity there shall be joy, and gladness, and praise. I AM SATISFIED. The reward is greater than was the deep anguish of the travail of My soul. Then will He say to His redeemed, "Come, ye blessed of My Father, inherit the kingdom prepared for you from the foundation of the world." Enter into your rest; the victory over sin and death is complete and eternal. "Receive the end of your faith, the salvation of your souls"—"an inheritance incorruptible, and undefiled, and that fadeth not away."

READER, two vital questions force themselves to the front.

"What think ye of Christ? Whose Son is He?" You reply, The Son of God, the Divine Redeemer. In this you say truly. What will you do with Christ? is the second great question. He is now offered to you, and you must decide. Will you receive and serve Him as your loved Lord and Saviour? Will you have Him as your eternal, unchangeable Friend? Or will you by neglect reject Him, and have Him for your judge and condemner? WHAT WILL YOU DO WITH JESUS OF NAZARETH?

www.ingramcontent.com/pod-product-compliance
Lightning Source LLC
Chambersburg PA
CBHW021156230426
43667CB00006B/420